May The Fathers Tell

By Andrew Burn

La'Mont Publications

May The Fathers Tell The Children
Copyright Andrew Burn November 2003.

ISBN 0–9545992–1–7

First Published November 2003
by La'Mont Publications

Printed in Great Britain for La'Mont Publications.

MAY THE FATHERS

TELL THE CHILDREN

FIGHTING WITH THE DESERT RATS, 1942 – 46

ANDREW BURN MC

K Battery

5th Royal Horse Artillery

MAY THE FATHERS TELL THE CHILDREN

FIGHTING WITH THE DESERT RATS, 1942 – 46

Andrew Burn MC

K Battery

5th Royal Horse Artillery

"May the Fathers long tell the children about this tale."

Churchill speaking to 7th Armoured Division, Berlin, 21 July 1945

"No Division has contributed more to the downfall of the Axis powers and to the total defeat of Germany.."

G.O.C. Major-General L.O.Lyne D.S.O. speaking of the 7th Armoured Division

For Lucy, William,
Miranda, Oliver, Sarah,
Philippa, Alistair, Anna,
Harriet, James, Sebastian,
Laurel, Katie, Elinor,
Nicholas, Hester, Aidan and
Noah.

Andrew Burn

Author's
Foreword

Everyone has their memories of the past and as time goes by these events seem to be more real than things that happened last month. So it was for me but I never thought of putting pen to paper until I happened to meet Tom Almond while cruising on the Upper Nile. He has had a background of studying and teaching English at Wolverhampton University and was very keen that I should try to put down on paper a record of these adventurous years of 1940 to 1946.

Up till now I have resisted any such ideas because they might be thought to be "blowing one's own trumpet" and even now I am worried that I might be doing this, knowing, as I do, how many people did so much more than I did and whose story needs to be told before mine.

However it is all nearly 60 years ago now and fast becoming ancient history.

Without Tom's encouragement I wouldn't have started and without his help and advice and that of John Buckley I wouldn't have kept going. I am very grateful to both of them.

I am also grateful to Andrea and to Trevanna for reading my manuscript and transferring it on to disk.

This book is dedicated to my grandchildren and I hope they and all my family will enjoy reading it and realise that everyone was young once.

Contents

1

Shipwreck

"All sunk beneath the waves
Fast by their native shore"
Cowper.

On Sunday, 6 August 1944 I, and a number of other wounded soldiers, were taken by amphibious DUKW down the lanes of Normandy, on to the beach and then into the sea when they transferred the propulsion from wheels to a propeller. We chugged out into deeper water where the hospital ship was at anchor. She was the SS Amsterdam, normally providing a ferry service from Harwich to the Hook of Holland. I have no idea of her tonnage but she was a sizeable vessel.

We tied up alongside; the stretcher cases were hoisted aboard and the walking wounded, of which I was one, came aboard under our own steam. It was then about 10pm and nearly dark and I was shown into a room where there were a number of steel cots bolted to the floor and I was allocated one of these and in due course took off my boots and trousers and went to bed. Next to me was an infantry subaltern who had lost both his legs and had been at the Field Hospital until he was strong enough for the journey home. We talked for some time and then went to sleep.

The next thing I knew was an enormous explosion and I saw my boots sliding across the deck and then, a moment later, sliding back again. I hurriedly put on my trousers and boots – a slightly longer operation than usual with one arm in a sling – and saw that there was no one left in our room except the subaltern in the next cot. Clearly he couldn't move and I couldn't lift him so I said that I would go and find help. I went up the companion way to the weather deck and saw that there was chaos. The ship was already listing heavily so that the lifeboats could not be lowered on the higher side and on the lower side people were doing their best to get the boats away. There was no hope of getting anyone to help me rescue my companion. I decided that I must go down and see him, so I made my way down again and told him that I could do nothing for him. What do you say to somebody in those circumstances? I think I just took his hand and bade him be of good courage – an emotional moment which still stays with me.

When I got home I made enquiries of the war office who were able to tell me his name and also the name of his next of kin – his parents. So I wrote to them and told them how their son had died and gave them some of the detail. I had a very nice reply from his mother who said that they had obviously been very distressed to hear of his injuries and had been looking forward to receiving him home and showing him their love.

By this time it was quite difficult getting up the companionway because of the list. On deck I could see that all the boats were away except for the stern one so I made my way into it. The reason that it had not got away was that the ship's list was so great that the davit at the stern end of the lifeboat was pushing it down and we could not get it away. No one seemed to be taking charge so I told everyone to move to the stern of the boat and try to depress it further from the davit, which was pushing it. Fortunately this worked and we were free. Just then the ship gave a lurch and I looked up and saw the funnel belching smoke and threatening to come down on top of us. I was also worried that if the ship went down quickly, as seemed likely, we might well go down with it since we were so close.

So I advised everyone who could swim to leave the lifeboat and swim away as far as they could and this is what I did myself. One can swim perfectly well without using one arm and I kicked off my boots and trousers to make it easier. After about twenty strokes I looked back and to my astonishment there was no ship – just an empty ocean with our lifeboat still afloat. It must have gone down very quickly and had not, after all, taken our lifeboat with it.

We were too concerned with our own survival to notice what was happening elsewhere but I learnt later that the ship had broken in two before it went down. My parents kept a press cutting from December 1944 (see page 10) which referred to this incident. There is no reference to the number of casualties but I think a great many must have lost their lives because being wounded they would not have been able to get up on deck. I heard it said that a lot of them were German wounded POW's, but I cannot confirm that. The press cutting states that it was a torpedo that caused the explosion, but it is unlikely that the enemy would torpedo a Hospital Ship in daylight (it was 5:30 am). We were told that it was an acoustic mine. There was nothing in the papers or on radio about the incident but bearing in mind press censorship and the need to maintain morale, this is not surprising.

So, going back to 7 August, here was I having a swim in the Channel on August Bank holiday. The water was not all that warm and there was not a lot of heat in the sun at 5:30 am so that when others pulled us back into the lifeboat we felt glad to be alive but unhappy to be so cold. Not long after that a Motor Torpedo Boat (MTB) took us on board and subsequently transferred us on to the *Duke of Lancaster*, which I think, was another Hospital Ship and in it we reached Portsmouth a few hours later. In addition to the embarrassment I felt about how insignificant my injuries were, there was the added problem that because I had no trousers I was deemed a stretcher case! and lying in an ambulance I was taken to a Canadian hospital in Haslemere, where they kept me for three days without either giving me any trousers or attending to my injuries. My letter home was written from this hospital and dated 9 August 1944.

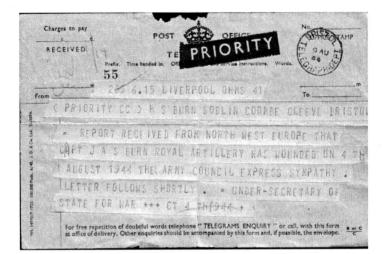

POST OFFICE TELEGRAPH

PRIORITY

Charges to pay
RECEIVED

Prefix. Time handed in. Office of Origin and Service Instructions. Words.

55

From 25 6.15 LIVERPOOL OHMS 41

PRIORITY CC H S BURN GODLIN COOMBE CLEEVE BRISTOL - REPORT RECEIVED FROM NORTH WEST EUROPE THAT CAPT J A S BURN ROYAL ARTILLERY WAS WOUNDED ON 4 TH AUGUST 1944 THE ARMY COUNCIL EXPRESS SYMPATHY . LETTER FOLLOWS SHORTLY . - UNDER-SECRETARY OF STATE FOR WAR +++ CT 4 TH 1944 +

For free repetition of doubtful words telephone " TELEGRAMS ENQUIRY " or call, with this form at office of delivery. Other enquiries should be accompanied by this form and, if possible, the envelope.

Hospital

Surrey

9ᵗʰ August 1944

Dear Mother & Father

Well I can continue my letter written from a hospital in France and tell you more – quite a lot more. But just in case you didn't get that letter, I will restate that I have received another small piece of shell fragment into my right shoulder from the front. It is still there, but as you can see from the unmarred beauty of the writing, the whole thing is slight. I will be going on very shortly from this hospital so I have given the county but not the number of the Hospital rather than vice-versa. Directly I get to a place where I am likely to stay, I will let you its full address immediately.

18

Now I will start with my story and so Antonio began. I left this hospital in the Bayeux area at 7 o'clock in the evening. I was definitely self-propelled and dressed with my arm in a sling. We went very slowly to the beach evacuation point where we dismounted. In due course we got onto DUKW and by this time, what with one thing and another, it was getting nearly dark. We went down to the sea were water borne and chugged out to the ship. The ship was lying a long way out and it took us quite a time to get there. Eventually we arrived and were hoisted aboard. Everything was very comfortable and I undressed and went to bed. In due course of time I went to sleep, and the next thing I remember is a most colossal explosion closely followed by another, things shot along the floor, windows broke, the ship shook – and I felt convinced that something had happened which wasn't altogether intended. Duly dossing my lifejacket I went up one flight of stairs, on to the deck, looked over the side and saw that the ship was undoubtedly sinking. I then returned to my deck, put on my boots and my battledress jacket and took a blanket quite forgetting that recently I had transferred my wallet back to my trousers – most irritating. By now the whole ship was listing horribly, walking on the deck was difficult enough, carrying a stretcher nearly impossible.

Back on deck again, I gave another chap a hand and then took a look round. Of the 4 boats that side, the side she was listing to, 2 had been smashed by the explosion, one was afloat and being loaded, the

20

other still only half full. I made the latter and got into it. Unfortunately the ship broke in two then and started to heel faster. The derrick that usually supports the boat was now pinning it down and starting to push it under water. We had to act quickly and got everyone in the boat up in the bow and so pushed the boat further down than the derrick and so freed it. We were still right alongside and now the ship was beginning to heel fast and the funnel seemed to be heading straight for us belching fire and brimstone. Now I didn't know what whirlpool effect there was when a biggish ship goes down, nor did I know whether the boilers would burst when the water got down the funnel so accordingly I left the boat and swam away about 25 yards and watched from there. Luckily

21

everything was all right so I then swam back to the boat. The whole process of the ship going down from the time when it was first hit was about 15 minutes. We had about 80 in our party. The remainder had got off the other side and after about 20 mins in the water were picked up by a Cruiser. We were picked up within 15 mins by an Motor Launch . I parked myself in the engine room and was quite warm. From there we were transferred to another Hospital ship. Altogether 20 crew, 40 wounded, 17 German wounded, the matron and 1 sister are believed to have been lost, which is small when everything is considered. A large number of these must have been killed by the initial explosion.

From the port we went by train to here, and tomorrow I think we will go on again.

I will try to get somewhere handy if I can possibly manage it.

On thinking things over I didn't lose an awful lot in wallet. There was £4, my driving licence, my identity card and some remaining clothing coupons. I will have to do a lot of buying of things like wallets, washing things, pants, shirts etc., but it might have been a lot worse. I think I will be able to get more coupons.

Hoping you are all well.

Much love,

Andrew

P.S. Let's have another early morning bathe off the coast of France, next August Bank Holiday!

On the Thursday I and a number of others were transferred on a train for the journey to Glasgow. I was

Nurses Rescue Wounded as their ship breaks in two

NURSES, doctors and orderlies who continued to help patients up on deck of the hospital carrier Amsterdam until the ship capsized, after she was torpedoed off Normandy on August 7, receive awards for their bravery in to-day's list.

When the ship turned over they escaped by scrambling down the almost horizontal side of the carrier just before she broke in two and sank.

Calmness Averted Panic

Three R.A.M.C. officers and three sisters of Queen Alexandra's Imperial Military Nursing Service have been awarded the M.B.E. and four men of the R.A.M.C. the B.E.M., the *London Gazette* announces.

The three sisters are Miss E. Roberts, of Formby, Lancs, Miss L. McNicholas, of Kiltimagh, Co. Mayo, and Miss E. T. Hourigan, of Ballinzarry, Co. Limerick.

Miss Roberts's calmness was an important factor in averting panic and "by her aid many patients reached the deck who would otherwise have been trapped," says the citation.

Unable to swim, Miss McNicholas became ill in the water, but as soon as she was rescued rendered first aid to patients.

The three doctors decorated are Capt. A. A. Grierson, of Wisborough Green, Sussex; Capt. C. T. A. Burgess, of Hoylake, Cheshire, and Lieut. G. Gray, of Haslemere, Surrey.

Made Stretcher Gangways

Trapped in his cabin by the explosion, Captain Grierson broke out and began to evacuate 100 patients. Handicapped by the loss of his glasses and injured, he was helping patients down the side as the ship sank.

Captain Burgess contrived gangways of stretchers from the deck to the water ambulances.

The ship broke through one of the wards on the lowest deck, of which Lieut. Gray was in charge, and sank while he was standing on the carrier's side trying to rescue through a porthole a trapped nursing officer.

Staff Sergeant B. Spink, of Armley, Leeds, and Sergt. A. W. Mitchell, of Rosehearty, Aberdeenshire, both worked in the wrecked ward through which the ship broke until every living patient had been moved.

24

still trouser-less and felt a complete fraud when WVS came round at station stops and gave us tea and buns and asked about our injuries.

Eventually we reached Killearn Hospital, not far from Glasgow, where the doctors were able to talk to me about my shoulder. Since, unlike Egypt two years earlier, there was no sign of infection they decided that the best thing to do was to leave it alone and let the fragment stay in my shoulder, where it still is and has caused no trouble.So my stay in hospital was fairly short and I went home on leave.

All this happened some years into the story I am about to tell. A story which begins in 1939 just as I was in my last year at school.

2

Early Days

"Happy the man whose wish and care
A few paternal acres bound"
Pope..

Britain declared war on Germany on 3 September 1939. I remember listening to Neville Chamberlain's broadcast and wondering what was going to happen now -- I was 17.

My parents, who had lived through the 1st World War, were dismayed. They had been through the horrors of that war and lost so many friends and relations and they could hardly bear the thought of a repetition. I realised that I was going to be involved in a major way. None of us thought it was going to last for nearly 6 years; in fact some of the papers were talking of it being over by Christmas! What we were actually experiencing was the end of one kind of world and the birth pains of another very different one.

My grandfather – my father's father – was a parish priest whose longest ministry was in the little village of Great Cheverell in Wiltshire. We all had a suspicion that he tried one or two other careers and when they were unsuccessful took Holy Orders as a last resort; but this may be grossly unfair. He was a good Vicar but a rather difficult man. When he was in his eighties and had to go into hospital for a dental operation my father picked him up in his car. He asked if he had got all that he needed for the hospital, to which his father asked "How should I know what I need having never been to hospital? I have my Bible, my toothbrush and a bottle of whisky and that should be enough".

He had four sons and two daughters and school fees were a problem. He wrote to all the schools on the Headmasters' Conference List and asked what discount they could offer for children of the clergy. Glenalmond in Scotland offered the biggest discount so my father and one of his brothers were sent there but my grandfather never visited the school before, during or after his sons were there. I also was sent there in 1935.

My father went from Glenalmond to Pembroke College, Cambridge to read engineering and then onto Sheffield to work for Messrs Firth & Son Steelmasters. During the 1st World War they were a vital part of the munitions industry and he was prevented from joining the forces as a result. In 1925 he moved south to Bristol as Chief Engineer of Imperial Tobacco Co (Comprising Wills and Players etc), which was then and for many years after a much-respected Bristol company - before anyone suspected a link between smoking and health. He bought a house and some land in Somerset in 1927 where he lived until his death in 1977. I am writing this from the same address as I had in those war time days and enjoy that wonderful sense of continuity that "a few paternal acres" can give.

There is little doubt in my mind that in my father's life from 1883 – 1977 he witnessed more technical innovations than any generation before or any subsequent generation is likely to. In my lifetime the only completely new innovation has been the computer; all the other incredible advances have been the development of previous discoveries. But in my lifetime there have been huge social changes. I have a feeling that life in 1930 was more similar to that in 1890 than 2002 is to 1930. As an illustration, our household in 1930 included two full time gardeners and four living-in domestic servants. There was a lot of formality and on every evening except Sunday the family dressed for dinner – and this meant dinner jackets – and we as children had to do the same once we had graduated from the nursery. The kitchen, scullery and pantry were not parts of the house that we went into often.

This whole idea of domestic service sounds strange to us today but it had its good points. Young girls after leaving school at the age of 14 would come to live in a large house and be given work for a very small wage but would have free board and lodging and would be provided with uniforms. There was quite a lot camaraderie "below stairs" and they learnt how the middle classes lived with new ideas in hygiene, cleanliness and orderliness. They would have a ½ day off per week and occasionally would be allowed a night at home. Normally they would leave to get married. We had one girl, Elsie Deacon, who started work with my parents in 1925 at the age of 19 and finally finished when my father died in 1977. She never married. She was genuinely part of the family. On one famous occasion in the 1960's when she happened to be with our household I passed the bedroom door one morning and heard my 5 year old son say "Elsie, I have wet my bed again" and she replied "Don't worry, I had the same trouble with your father!"

The system of early schooling in those days was with a Private Governess. If one family in the vicinity had the wealth and size of house they would employ a

Governess who lived in permanently - in an awkward position of below "upstairs" and above "downstairs". In order to give her a reasonable size of class, in addition to the child or children of the family, selected neighbours would be asked to let their children join the class if their ages were right. In this way my elder sister and I were invited and we walked across the two fields that separated us from the big house and had our lessons there - and very good they were too. I was doing Latin at age seven and was well ahead of the rest when I went off to my boarding Prep school at eight.

Leaving home at 8 seems cruel by today's standards but it was the accepted norm in those days. The first term away was not too bad because there was an element of novelty in it but we were all homesick to some extent and longed for our mother's support. Going back to school for the second and later terms was more painful but one had to accept that you lived two lives, one at home and one at school. I recall one amusing conversation from when I was 8 or 9. A number of us were trying to establish how babies were born or more precisely how they were conceived. A number of wild ideas were canvassed and then one boy – Carter – came up with what we later on realised was the right answer and we laughed him to scorn for coming up with so ridiculous an idea. I suppose that none of us were brought up on farms.

There was at that time the much recorded gulf between the gentry on the one side and the working class on the other. I remember one delightful incident when I had committed a car parking offence in September 1939 when a car park in Bristol had ceased to be a car park and I had not noticed the signs. The village policeman brought the summons by hand but, not wishing to embarrass me, he waited at the bottom of the drive for hours until we went out by car and then came up to the house and handed it to the cook. The war succeeded in closing this gulf – though class has remained a preoccupation of the English.

Indeed one 'benefit' which followed the outbreak of war was the cohesion it brought to the community. We were less than five hundred in our village but my mother claimed that she knew everyone. There was a lot of contact between households – often standing in the inevitable queue for shopping – and families whose fathers had gone to the war would be helped and cared for by neighbours. There were only a few cars on the road because of petrol rationing and every driver would fill his car with people waiting at the bus stop.

The most immediate effect on the village was the call to accommodate the large number of mothers and children evacuated into the country from the East End of London. My mother was in charge of this at our end and my sister and I spent many hours visiting the farms and houses to see how many each was able to receive. The evacuees arrived late one evening and the organization sprang into action. We had two families in our house – one from Poplar in London and the other from Bristol. Many returned to London after a few weeks because

London at that time seemed fairly safe. Eventually the few families that wanted to stay were housed together in a large house in the village that happened to be unoccupied. A lady was found to look after it and she remained there for all of the war. Fortunately she was a lady of independent means and this was her contribution to the war effort.

Of the two families that were in our house, the ones upstairs were the Pratts from Poplar. They had the old nursery, which, although it was on the upper floor, had a door out into the garden because the house was on a hillside. They also had a bathroom, a separate w. c. and one bedroom, which used to be the cook's. The family was the mother and her two children. They cooked on a paraffin stove. The other family was called Holmyard and they were from Bristol. They had our drawing room by the front door and also the cloakroom and w.c. They were, I think, a man and wife without children. They also cooked on a paraffin stove and all their washing was done in a small hand basin in the cloakroom. The hot water in the house came from a solid fuel boiler in the scullery which was lit every afternoon to provide hot water in the evening and then left to burn itself out. Our own kitchen had an Esse solid fuel cooker which was very similar to an AGA and was introduced about the same time. My father brought it in 1936, my wife and I converted it to oil in 1960 and my son and daughter-in-law are still using it.

The first nine months of the war came to be known as the Phoney War and it did not impact too much on people's lives apart from the inevitable rationing of most commodities. But in May 1940 it all changed with the German invasion of the Low Countries and France and the eventual British escape via Dunkirk. As events unfolded we all came to realize that we were living in momentous times. In June 1940 Churchill, in one of his famous speeches, referred to the real danger of a descent "into the abyss of a new Dark Age" if the Germans were not resisted and I remember walking the hills of Perthshire wondering if civilisation – our country and myself – would survive the next five years. We all came to the conclusion that we must come forward and make whatever contribution we could to the best of our abilities.

In the previous January I had travelled from Glenalmond to Oxford to sit for a Scholarship in Classics. In those days you had to go to the University and sit the exam in their premises. One of the exams was in the Hall of Balliol College. It was a freezing cold day and the only heating was from two coal fires. My fingers were dead as I wrestled with a Latin unseen. As a result I was not awarded a scholarship but was offered a place at Trinity to read Law in October 1940. The arrangement at that time was that if you had a university place you could take it up but only for two years. After this you had to join the forces like everyone else. I thought about this carefully and decided that I could always go up to university after the war – if all went well – but that my real place in 1940 was with the forces, so I turned down the offer of a place.

I came home at the end of June and found that the Army would not take young men under the age of 18 but Young Soldiers Battalions were being formed and I could join in early September. In the meantime I joined the Local Defence Volunteers – subsequently known as the Home Guard. This was an organization, which, on the face of it, was every bit as ridiculous as that portrayed in "Dad's Army". But two important things need to be said. First, it gave the population, primarily the men, an opportunity to do something rather than wait for other people, even if that something was ludicrously inadequate; and second it confirmed, or helped to confirm, the vital fact that the population of this country intended to resist invasion and not surrender.

We had no weapons so my father obtained some buckshot for his twelve bore shotgun and decided to try it out on our tennis court. He obtained some large sheets of white cardboard and on these drew the outline of an enemy soldier and hung them on the wire netting. We then fired on these from different distances and counted the number of hits on each outline. The conclusion was that we would have to be fairly close to do any real damage. Fortunately it was never put to the test.

Apart from making plans to form a roadblock on the main road, one special job was to man an observation post on the nearest hill to look out for enemy parachutists. Four of us would form the team and a hut, with two bunks, was erected at the observation point where we did two hours on and two hours off. It was a wonderful place to be on a summer's night. We saw some wildlife but no enemy. We did, however, on one occasion have a view across the Bristol Channel of the bombing of Cardiff. It was like a distant spectacular firework display with the awful realization of the damage and casualties being caused.

The threat of invasion was very real and my father - always anticipating future problems – concealed various essentials in the garden. Behind one wall was a can of petrol and hidden in the cleft in the rock in another part was a tobacco tin with £10 in cash. It was quite a few years later that he remembered the tin of money and recovered it. This sum doesn't sound very much but if you compare it on the basis of a private soldier's pay which was two shillings per day in 1940 and £143 per week today, then £10 is the equivalent of £2000.

Early in September, aged just eighteen, I and my nearest neighbour David Sinclair joined the Young Soldiers' Battalion of the Glosters and went to their barracks in Gloucester where for nearly two months we had the normal training and drill of a new recruit. The pay was two shillings and six pence a day (twelve and a half pence in present currency) and we lived on that without accepting any subsidy from home. It was quite a challenge with our different backgrounds to relate effectively with the other recruits but we managed it and enjoyed those few weeks.

Our sleeping accommodation was in bunks in what used to be a garage and in the next bunk to me was a farmer's boy from the Forest of Dean. He was fascinated by me changing my clothes when I went to bed and he asked what it was I was putting on. When I told him they were pyjamas, he said he had never heard of these. He also asked me on one occasion how many baths per week I usually had. Because it was my custom then – and still is today – to start the day with a cold bath and always to finish it with a hot one, I said fourteen. He was speechless!

On the face of it this entry into a completely different circle of people might have been difficult to handle but there are two points to bear in mind – first everyone else was in the same boat. We had all just arrived from our civilian occupations and were being "broken in" to army life – in many cases it was the first occasion when many of them had been away from home. It wasn't as though we were joining an established group of people who would collaborate in taking the mickey out of us; and second, David and I had experienced this once or twice before when we went off to boarding school.

Whatever the reasons we all succeeded in enjoying ourselves. We had joined the army to defend our country and were mortified early in September when codeword "Cromwell" was proclaimed as an indication of imminent invasion and we were confined to barracks "in case we should come to some harm"!

3

Officer Cadet

"Land of our birth we pledge to thee
Our love and toil in the years to be"
Kipling.

Early in October I applied for a new course introduced
by the War Office whereby young men of my age with
the necessary academic qualifications could be sent to a
university for a six month Course and then to an Officer
Cadet Training Unit (OCTU) with a view to being given
a commission in the Sappers, Gunners or Signals. I
opted for the Gunners and was accepted for the first
Course.

We all assembled at Harrogate before going on to the
University chosen for us (in my case Edinburgh) and I
remember nearly falling for one of the oldest Army
tricks when the Sergeant called for five volunteers who
had passed their driving test. I had passed mine but held

back from coming forward because of a vague suspicion, but five others came forward and were immediately told to go out and clean the latrines!

Edinburgh was a very enjoyable interlude. We were in civilian clothes again and were not worked too hard. There was time for sport, some social life and the theatres were all open as though there was no war. We had all come from public schools and in fact one of our number had been at my prep school in the early 1930s so we had no difficulty in getting on with each other. A number of theatres put on shows that had moved out of London and I remember particularly seeing Ivor Novello's *Dancing Years*. Edinburgh is a wonderful city and we made the most of it. It was one of the few occasions in the war when, as far as I was concerned, we were able to enjoy the company of girls. Apart from this and one or two leaves in 1944 I spent the years between 18 and 24 with virtually no social life.

On one occasion a very much older cousin – Kenneth Atkinson – who was Commander of the battleship *HMS*

Nelson wrote to me to say that his ship was at Rosyth for a few days and would I come to dinner on board. I got the invitation extended to include Robin Forestier-Walker, who had a motorbike, and we rode to S. Queensferry where the motorboat was waiting for us. We dined in great state on this huge vessel. Sadly my cousin was subsequently appointed Captain of the dockyard at Singapore and did not survive the Japanese invasion.

After Edinburgh we had six weeks at an OR (other ranks) training Establishment at Aldershot mainly for the benefit of those of our number who had not served in the Army before Edinburgh, and then on to our OCTU at Catterick. The Camp was out in the countryside not far from Richmond and the barracks were newly built; they were called Belisha Blocks after Mr Hore-Belisha who was Secretary of State for the war in the mid thirties – the same man that gave his name to the Pedestrian Crossings.

The two months at Catterick were fairly intensive but enjoyable as there was a lot to learn about Gunnery and the way an Artillery Regiment operated. One of the requirements was that everyone should be competent in driving a vehicle and suitable instruction was given. Since I and a few others already had their driving licences we were taught to ride motorcycles across country and this was a wonderful experience over moor land and in and out of ditches. The nearest town to Catterick Camp was Richmond and this is a beautiful place with lots of character. The countryside round about is also glorious and as we drove around on our exercises in lovely summer weather bringing our guns into action and practicing all the skills we were going to need, we couldn't help wondering what the future held for our beautiful country.

At the end of the Course I was appointed Senior Under Officer (SUO) and took command of the whole parade at the passing out ceremony on the very large Parade Ground. I was out in front and had to give the command to "Present Arms" as soon as the Colonel arrived at the saluting base. Unfortunately on that morning there was a very thick mist so that I could see neither the saluting base nor the troops behind me and they couldn't see me. All I could do was to listen for the Colonel's footsteps – my hearing was better then than it is now! – and as soon as they stopped give the necessary commands. I think I got it about right.

Towards the end of our course at Catterick we were asked to express our preferences for which branch of Artillery we wished to join. There was quite a wide spread between the Royal Horse Artillery (RHA), Field Artillery, Medium, Anti-aircraft, Anti-tank, etc., etc. The most prestigious was the RHA and many people put this as their first choice with two or three further choices. With a certain amount of bravado and a not very likeable conceit, I put RHA first and a line through any further choices. It was a bit of a game really but it worked and I got my posting to 5th RHA as a 2nd

Lieutenant and stayed with them for the whole of the active war. It was 4 October 1941.

The RHA is part of the Royal Regiment of Artillery which comprised a great variety of different types of gunnery. From the earliest days there were always guns in any British Army and gradually they became more mobile and were able to move with the cavalry and come into action quickly. In the RHA they came to be known by the letter of their troop and were awarded as battle honours the name of the place where they had distinguished themselves or by their commander. RHA were very active in Wellington's Armies in Spain, Portugal and also at Waterloo. In 5 RHA one of our Batteries was G (Mercer's Troop) named after Captain Mercer who commanded the guns at Waterloo. There are many other names such as Rocket Troop, Chestnuts, Sphinx, Nery etc. At the time I joined them they were generally being allocated to Armoured Divisions, but this was not a hard and fast arrangement.

RHA had a different cap badge to RA but in training and establishment they were hardly distinguishable from the RA Field Regiment. There was a slight elitism in RHA and an element of competition in getting posted there. After about a year a young subaltern, if he had performed well, would be awarded his 'jacket' and authorised to wear the ball buttons which were unique to RHA and to wear the cap badge.

123 O.C.T.U,1941

2nd Lieutenant Andrew Burn is Third From The Right

In The Front Row

4

North African Posting

"The lone and level sands stretch far away"
Shelley.

When I joined the 5th RHA they were in Gomshall
Surrey and the Regimental HQ was in a large house
called Rounddown and the Batteries G, K and CC in
neighbouring villages. K battery had recently been
given the battle honour of "Hondeghem Troop" after a
particularly gallant action at a village of that name in
1940 shortly before the Dunkirk evacuation. The
Commanding Officer was Lieutenant Colonel Rawdon
Hoare, a cousin of Sir Samuel Hoare (Foreign Secretary
1935). He was something of a martinet and you had to
watch your step very carefully. At that time the officers
wore the same battledress as other ranks but whereas
theirs was buttoned up to the neck, officers wore them
with the top buttons undone and a collar and tie beneath.

The CO thought this untidy and we were the only regiment in the Army whose Officers wore their battledress buttoned up to the neck. In the second week we had a formal dinner with guests but I was told that since our number would be thirteen and the CO would not sit down thirteen to dinner, I, as the most junior officer would have to go out to the nearest pub for a meal and could join the dinner at the Port stage. You just had to do what you were told!

Soon after joining I was sent for two weeks on a Survey Course at Larkhill, near Salisbury. Surveying in the guns was an important speciality for an Artillery Regiment since the accuracy with which the guns engage targets is very dependent on how accurately they are surveyed in to the map and how parallel to each other the guns are. The teaching we had received at Edinburgh was helpful in understanding what we had to learn at Larkhill and it was this Course that qualified me to be appointed as Regimental Survey Officer in December 1942.

It might be helpful to explain why the Regiment needed a Survey Officer. The basic system of operation of a regiment of field guns (25 pdrs) – the Regiment had 3 Batteries and each Battery had 2 Troops - was to bring the guns into action with each troop of four guns as the smallest operative unit; the other troop in the Battery was always fairly close but the two other Batteries might be as much as a mile away. Orders to fire usually originate from the Forward Observation Officers (FOOs) who frequently call for fire by using the map reference of the target they wish to engage. As their title suggests these officers are in forward positions where they can see the enemy and therefore are able to call for fire as required. The FOO's position was often exposed and there were many casualties. It was therefore important if the fire was to be accurate that the guns should be surveyed in so that the calculations would be right; it was also important that if they came into action with a "zero line" of say 100 degrees (East of North) then each gun must be accurately aligned on this bearing. To do this the Survey Officer had to establish a position and an alignment as accurately as he could – or make use of Divisional Survey Information – and then pass this line and position to each Battery as quickly and as accurately as he could. The instruments he had were a "Director", which resembled a theodolite, a range finder, measurement tapes and banderols (survey poles). His team consisted of two light trucks and about eight men, one of whom would be a Bombardier (NCO with two stripes).

On one occasion when I was doing this job in the desert I had considerable difficulty establishing exactly where I was, but since it was more important in that sort of terrain to get the Batteries shooting together than taking hours to set up the map reference exactly right, I made an informed guess and passed it around the Batteries with normal survey techniques. A little later one of the Batteries reported to me that the position I had given him put him one hundred yards out to sea! So it was back to the drawing board!

We stayed in Surrey until we embarked for Africa in early May of the following year, 1942 and our time was spent in concentrated training in the surrounding areas. Some of the Officers and many of the men had been involved in the fighting in France in May 1940 and their experience and the general air of competence in the Regiment was very impressive. A young 2nd Lieutenant has as much to learn from the men he commands as from the senior Officers to whom he is responsible and the other ranks were always helpful to their officers as long as the latter didn't pretend that they knew all the answers.

When the young subaltern joins his regiment for the first time he has had the basic training from his OCTU but he has a lot more to learn not only about the handling of his guns but more importantly the handling of his men. His NCOs and warrant officers are all much more experienced than he is. If he is wise he will not try to pretend otherwise until he has 'caught up'. Gradually he will form an opinion on the strengths and weaknesses

54

of his men and will be able to exert some leadership, but he must earn their trust and respect first.

There was an example of this when we first were reunited with our guns in Egypt in June 1942. We were required to give the guns a major check to ensure that they were in perfect condition and while this work was going on I was moving from gun to gun observing what was going on but not really performing any function. One of the sergeants – Hooley – was No.1 of his gun and I knew him to be a reliable and intelligent man. Due to an oversight he left out an important plug in the oil recoil system so that when he elevated the gun the oil drained out rapidly and the barrel – or piece – slid back off its runners – a near disaster for which Hooley could have been severely reprimanded. I saw this but no other officer did. The proper thing was for me to report this incident to my superior officer but I formed the opinion that it was a careless slip and not all that blameworthy. So after establishing with Hooley that he was duly contrite I kept quiet about the incident and as a result my relationship with the men became noticeably easier.

It was about this time that I came to hear about General Montgomery. He was Corps Commander of South Eastern Command – a Lieutenant General – and was already making his presence felt. Among other things he insisted on physical fitness and everyone from senior officer to private soldier was ordered to take regular exercise and, in particular, be able to run something like three miles in half an hour (I don't remember the exact details). Anyone unable to do this was reported. As a result of this directive, a number of the more elderly officers had to leave the division. On one occasion he summoned all the officers in his command to a "Pep" talk in a cinema in Brighton. We came from all directions and sat spellbound as he gave one of his homilies. It was all very effective and we came away enthused and determined to "fight the good fight".

Monty's character and mannerisms have been studied as much as anyone's and it is difficult to establish why he went down so well with the men under his command. He seemed to have the same way of relating to men – but probably not to women! – as Baden Powell did to his Boy Scouts. He did not talk down to us – he exuded enthusiasm and he gave the impression, which was probably a true one, that he really knew what he was talking about. He had studied the art of war and of leadership and it came across loud and clear.

Early in 1942 I was transferred to K Battery and became the Troop Leader of E/F Troop. Our guns were the ubiquitous 25 pounders – at that time towed behind their limber and the Quad. This was an enclosed four-wheel drive vehicle accommodating the gun crew and all their equipment. There were four guns per troop and two Troops per Battery. The number of men in the Troop was about seventy-five.

The 25 pdr was the standard field gun in the British Army for the whole war. Not all the regiments had it in France in 1940 but from then on it became the standard weapon. It was reliable and fairly accurate but its 25 pound shell came to be seen as too light and after the war a heavier gun took its place. It was technically a gun/howitzer with separate shell and cartridge. There was a choice of 4 different charges 1, 2, 3 and supercharge and the choice was made by taking out one or more coloured bags of cordite from the brass cartridge or, in the case of supercharge, adding a fourth one. Maximum range was 13,400 yards with supercharge. When brought into action its wheels were located on a large horizontal circular frame so that the gun could be swung around 360° by hand.

We were at that time part of 8th Armoured Division whose sign was the word "GO" on a green background – like the traffic light. The Division was being sent out to Egypt and we embarked at Liverpool at the beginning of May. All the Units were split up between the ships and K Battery was separate from the rest of 5RHA on a magnificent vessel called the Monarch of Bermuda, which had been built for the New York – Bermuda trip particularly to attract passengers who wanted a cruise holiday with no restrictions on alcohol at the time of Prohibition in the USA.

There were about 3000 troops on board and though there was some congestion I was lucky in sharing a cabin with two others with "en suite" facilities. There were restrictions on the use of fresh water but we were issued with salt-water soap so that we could wash in sea water. All the original ship's staff were still on duty and we had white-jacketed stewards to serve us with our meals and the food was very good.

Catering arrangements for the other ranks were rather more congested. They were fed in three sittings so it was important to get each sitting in and out exactly on time for each meal – about a thousand men each sitting. I was appointed one of the messing officers and was involved every day in overseeing this procedure. Occasionally the Field Officer of the day – a Major – would come down to inspect and I remember one amusing incident when an irate private soldier at the inaccessible end of the table held up his plate complaining of a beetle in his potato – the other members of the table were supporting him and angry. The Major squeezed up to the end of the table, looked closely at the potato and said in a very audible whisper "Shut up, you fool, or they will all be wanting one!" This was a good example of the role of humour in dealing with awkward situations – an outlet much used in the dangerous months to come.

I do not know the route the convoy took but I think we went West across the Atlantic before turning South down the Eastern Seaboard of the U.S. and crossing Eastwards for our first landfall at Freetown in Sierra Leone, where we did not disembark. We were quite a large convoy of mainly liners with a strong destroyer escort. At Freetown we had the Mother and Father of a thunderstorm and the Troops – fed up with washing in salt-water, came on deck with their bars of soap and had a good wash and shower in the torrential rain. To the best of my belief there were no women on board!

After a very short stop we travelled south and our next stop was Cape Town. I had a wonderful dawn view of Table Mountain silhouetted against the rising sun as we approached. Here we were allowed ashore for about three days. Fortunately one of our Officers – Chris North had his home in Cape Town and his family really pushed the boat out to entertain us and we had a wonderful day or two. Sadly Chris was later killed in Italy. Adderly Street is still the main street of Cape Town, but in those days it ran right down to the harbour and you found yourself in the heart of the city as soon as you left the Dock Gates. In 1942 it was a city for the whites and the native Africans were in a subservient position, but there was no noticeable tension. The local – white – population went out of their way to receive and entertain the troops with great generosity and warmth and everyone had very happy memories when we rejoined our ships and went on northwards up to the Eastern Coast of Africa.

The only military operation during those few days was two nights in a tented camp at a place called Retreat – south of the city. Today this is a built up area with thousands of houses, but in 1940 it was unspoilt country with trees and fields. On the last morning I had to get up very early to take a party of men who had been on guard duty the night before back to the ship on foot. I think it was about four miles and this would not have been too much of a problem except that it chose to rain as hard as I have ever seen it and by the time we reached the train and the ship we were like drowned rats.

As we left Cape Town Harbour we had a sight of the *RMS Queen Elizabeth* coming in. She was a huge vessel and coming in very fast. She always travelled without escort and relied on her speed to keep clear of enemy attack.

Our next port of call was Aden but we were there only for a short time and did not go ashore. The rest of the Convoy was on its way to India and the escort went with them. We made our way individually and fairly fast up the Red Sea to Port Taufiq, which is in effect the southern end of the Suez Canal. There we disembarked and went by rail to El Tahag which is midway between Cairo and Ismailia where we were reunited with our vehicles and guns. It was the first week of July 1942. Our base at Tahag was a tented camp in desert type of terrain and very hot. I remember putting some water into my canvas washing basin and then being called away. When I returned an hour or so later the water was too hot for my hands.

The situation in Egypt at that time was critical; Rommel had pushed the 8th Army back to the edge of the Delta and the question was whether or not we could prevent him from pushing us back further. The fighting had been going on in the Western Desert for two years. To begin with the British pushed the Italians west as far as Benghazi but then the Germans sent forces into the area to reinforce the Italians. We were forced back to the Egyptian border but held on to Tobruk. A subsequent offensive forced the enemy back again towards

Benghazi but a counter attack by Rommel and fearsome battles around Sidi Rezegh resulted in the 8th army retreating to the edge of the Delta.

This was the occasion for Churchill's visit and Montgomery's appointment as Army Commander. We were very much new boys trying to learn as quickly as possible the techniques of desert warfare. After a relatively short time our Division was moved up into action on the Ruweisat Ridge for the first contact with the enemy. On our way we drove past the Pyramids and into the very hot and dry desert. There were obviously no roads but the Military Police had established various tracks, which were well marked and used for safe travel between minefields. Away from these tracks one tended to navigate by compass and most vehicles had a sun-compass on the roof of their cab that would be set for the required bearing and time of day. The combination of this and the milometer on the dashboard was quite effective.

On nearly the first day of our arrival in the Battlezone I was told to take an important message to Brigade headquarters and given a map reference of their location. It was the end of the day and getting dark as I set off in my truck. Unfortunately I had been given the map reference of their previous location and not of their present one. Nearly every track we followed had minefields either side indicated only by one strand of wire about a foot from the ground. As it became darker it was increasingly difficult to follow instructions to find brigade headquarters and also to see the minefields. Eventually I delivered the message and then had to find our way back. By now it was quite dark but there was a moon. We had travelled most of the way back when the moon set and it was pitch dark and pointless to go on. So we stopped and dossed down and had no trouble in making our way back at first light. I don't think my crew enjoyed the outing any more than I did!

Our Armoured Regiments were equipped at this time with Valentine tanks which were not very effective and whose guns were too small. We gave artillery support to a number of minor attacks which did not achieve their objective and we were at the receiving end of some enemy counter-battery fire. Being fairly new to the game we made an error by firing on an enemy target after dark one evening and then not leaving our position at first light, as we should have done. The enemy flash-spotters had taken a bearing on us and early next morning sent over some very accurate gunfire, which knocked out one of our guns and caused several casualties of which I was one. I had a small shell splinter in my left leg and some superficial grazing to my chest. I didn't think it was very serious, but they insisted on evacuating me to Regimental Aid Post. It was from here I wrote a letter home.

24/7/42

Dear Mother and Father

There is a bigger lapse between this letter and the last than usual, but things have been moving a little more quickly. We left our camp and came up nearer the front. I might say in passing that we came through Cairo. Compared with the deserted and deadly sort of country round about it, it is really a sight for sore eyes. I think that if and when I get any leave, I will be able to enjoy myself in Cairo. There is a club there with swimming pools, tennis courts and gallons of stuff to drink which, when you feel hot, dry and thirsty, fairly makes your mouth water.

We came up by road and stayed nights at different places. We now do all our cooking and eating by vehicles. Each truck is given its rations and it cooks its own meals which isn't usually very difficult since it is mostly tinned. It generally consists of little more than boiling water to make some tea. But on the whole we feed quite well. It is surprising what good things you can get out of a tin.

We are in action now, and things are exactly the same as manoeuvres and exercises in England, except that one has to be a little more careful about things. No lights of course are allowed; it is quite all right at the moment because there is a bright moon but when there is none and everything is pitch dark, it is going to be very tricky indeed. It is quite incredible how easy it is to get lost our here; there are no landmarks at all, and if you start using patches of scrub as landmarks, then you will get on to the wrong one next time and will lose yourself completely. It took me once from 7 o'clock in the evening till 11.30 to find a unit that was only 4 miles away! And I once lost myself for 10 minutes over a distance of 500 yards.

We have done quite a bit of firing and we hope that we have done a lot of damage. We think we have but you can never tell for certain. I am writing this sitting on my camp bed just beside an ambulance; the reason being as follows: A few stray German shells came over in our direction the day before yesterday and one came unfortunately close. As I was going down to flatten myself on the ground 3 small pieces shot past in front of me. One took my breast pocket away but didn't touch my body at all, the second did exactly the same with my right trouser pocket, and the third and smallest hit my left thigh; the cut is minute but it has bruised my thigh a bit and so my leg is a little stiff. So I am being sent back for a 2 day rest.

Otherwise I am quite well, so for Lord's sake don't exaggerate (I am not minimising!).

I have had no letters from you yet, so please send by airmail, air postcards or airgraphs or something. I have given up writing ordinary letters, they take too long. I am longing to hear some news about the family but I doubt if it will be long now before they all arrive.

One only gets one of these letter cards a week, so I cannot send them everywhere. I forgot to write to Mary for her birthday. I only remembered on July 4th, so please apologise for me. I think I may succeed in remembering Christmas.

Much love, Andrew

The shelling had, in fact, been quite frightening. When I stood up after it was over I saw one of my men dead and one with his hand blown off. Three of our four guns were unharmed but the fourth had received a lot of damage with 2 of the crew wounded and one dead. I went over to the gun to organise appropriate action including the replacement of one of its wheels, which had been punctured, when I was summoned back to the Command Post "at the walk" and told to report to the Medical Officer.

As so often happens one feels worse after a few hours than at the time and I was sent further back through the medical channels, first to Alexandria and then to El Tahag, where we had been a few weeks before. Although the wound seemed to be very minor it became infected because the splinter had taken some clothing into the wound with it and it was over three months before I left the hospital having been moved from Egypt to Palestine where our hospital was at BIR Yakov near Sarafand. If they had had penicillin I would have been back in half the time.

5

Hospital in Palestine

Quinquireme of Nineveh from distant Ophir
Rowing home to haven in sunny Palestine
Masefield.

My letter of 3rd October shows that I was getting rather frustrated:

3/10/42

> *Dear Mother and Father*
>
> *Mail is getting strung up again and I haven't had any for about a week; in fact not since I acknowledged your last lot. It's very annoying because both the places that it may have got stuck at, do actually know where I am, but no doubt it will turn up sooner or later.*
>
> *Very little has turned up and it is no easy task writing a letter in hospital with*

nothing to answer. My wound is healing up very nicely now, in fact the smaller part of it has healed right over. The rest ought to take about a fortnight more. I will then go to a convalescence depot for about another fortnight and by then I ought to be ready for the fray again. The other chap who is in with me used to gloat over the fact that he would be out before me, but now I think I will beat him.

I awoke last night at about 1 o'clock to hear the first rain that I have heard since June 10th; what a country! It was very pleasant and when I woke up there was that lovely smell you get in England in summer after a short shower. It was lovely.

I am still wandering round on crutches but every evening now I go out for a stroll round the neighbouring grounds and have a look at the oranges that aren't yet ripe and other various things; it is very annoying to be in a place and not know much more than you can see from your bed. After much pestering for fresh fruit we yesterday got some bananas and a few unripe oranges; and in the evening a sister brought me a fresh date. I was amazed to find that although the skin looked smoother and shinier the taste was exactly the same as any you would find in a box in England. The figs will be ripe soon and then nothing can hold me back!

(later)

Little to write home about! except the weather. This afternoon we had a magnificent storm; it started with a strong wind and then "the rains came". The tent below us was blown right in and a few beds belonging to convalescing patients were completely covered. The rains were accompanied by thunder in the true Indian novel tradition. I only wish the oranges would ripen. I got a very green one yesterday, cut it in half and squeezed the juice out. Surprisingly enough the juice was very nearly the same as that of a ripe orange; it had the same sweet taste and yet was very bitter which seems a bit of a paradox but is true.

Still no more mail, curse someone!

Am longing to get back to the Regt.

Much love,

Andrew

Palestine seemed very relaxed and orderly at that time. Tel Aviv and Jaffa were one conurbation with Jews in Tel Aviv and Arabs in Jaffa but there did not appear to be much tension. The only other place I went to after leaving hospital was a rehabilitation centre at Natanya where all the Cavalry horses had been sent after mechanization. In an effort to get fit again I spent most days riding around the countryside.

Bearing in mind all that has happened to Palestine and to the Jews in Europe since 1948 it is interesting to recall how relaxed things were at this time. We were aware of the political campaign for a Jewish state but there was no evidence of serious unrest and we were not aware then of the terrible things happening to the Jews in Europe. We knew Hitler was violently anti-Semitic but had no inkling of the horrors of the holocaust that were to come. In a way there was good evidence of the Pax Britannica at work.

This was the time when the Battle of Alamein was starting. We all knew that Monty planned a great attack but we did not know when this would happen. The first requirement was to withstand Rommel's attack which came at Alam Halfa on 30 August. Monty had anticipated this with uncanny accuracy and the attack was repulsed with heavy enemy losses. The imperative now was to build up the allied forces with more men, more tanks and more guns and to organise a plan of deception which would lead the enemy to misjudge where the weight of the allied attack would come. The front was fairly narrow – it was limited at the north end by the sea and at the south by the Qattara Depression which was impassable soft sand. Monty bided his time as he amassed considerable superiority in men, guns and tanks – 1200 tanks to Rommel's 485.

The outcome of this battle was so important to all of us that we listened for every scrap of news after it had started. The opening shots of the battle were fired on 23 October and the final breakthrough by the 7th Armoured Division was on 2 November; so it took 10 days of fierce fighting before it was over. The result, as we know, was the first major allied victory of the war. We were clearly disappointed at not being with our regiments but there was nothing we could do about it except make all speed and rejoin them as soon as we were fit. We were thrilled to hear later on that the church bells in England were rung to celebrate the victory. They had been silent for two years because they were to be the signal of a German invasion and were only to be rung in this eventuality. It was also at this time that Churchill in addressing the Lord Mayor's Banquet said that the victory of Alamein "was not the end, nor even the beginning of the end, but might safely be called the end of the beginning".

After my convalescence in Natanya I returned to Cairo by train and to the RA Depot where I found a fellow Officer from the Regiment, Denys Benke, also trying to get back. It wasn't as easy as we anticipated. The Battle of Alamein was now over and the 8th Army was in pursuit westwards but the CO of the depot was unwilling to let us go before the paperwork was in order. In the end we forced his hand and having found a convoy of 1000 men due to leave for the front the next day we told him that we were going with it. There were something like forty 3-ton trucks with the men packed into them and all under the command of two Subalterns recently arrived from the UK. Denys warned them before we started that it was dangerous to put the Cook's truck at the back of the Convoy in case it broke down but the inexperienced subalterns didn't reorganise the convoy and by the time we reached Mersa Matruh on the first evening there was no Cook's truck and no food – it had broken down. So here we were with 1000 men and no food - and it was raining! Denys, who was a Captain at that stage, told the Subaltern that we would take charge. He said that he would pacify the men and told me to take a truck and go and get one day's rations for 1000 men – just like that.

I found a Military Policeman who directed me to the nearest RASC (Royal Army Service Corps) depot and I went there. The depot commander, who was a Major, told me that without specific authorization he could not give me any rations. I again explained the situation but he wouldn't relent – so I tried a bit of play-acting. I took out my notebook and asked for his initials, name and Army number. He asked why I wanted it and I replied that when I reported the Major's refusal to my Brigadier I wanted to make sure I had the correct details. There was a pause and he gave me the authorization!

Having dealt with this problem, Denys and I decided to go off on our own. It was quite easy to hitch hike on one of the supply lorries since each of these lorries had only one driver with a spare seat next to him and since we were of Commissioned rank we could virtually insist.

So my next lift took me as far as Tobruk where a local Infantry Regt HQ fed me and gave me a place to sleep. Next morning they lent me a Jeep and 'driver' for half an hour so that I could find my next lift. This turned out to be a Convoy of lorries taking bombs up to the forward air base. The bombs – maybe 250lbs each – were stacked on a sloping hillside and the trucks were backed up to the pile and the tailboard lowered. The men then rolled the bombs down the hill and up into the truck! They had nearly finished when I came on the scene and very soon we set off westwards again. I spent two days with this convoy and since it rained spent a very cold night sleeping on the bombs in the back of the truck. This convoy was not going any further than Benghazi so I was on the lookout for another which was going further west; this turned out to be a food convoy and I went on with them. We were now getting close to the rear echelons of the Division and I spotted our Regimental sign on the side of the track and got out with my bedding roll. The Regimental Quarter-Master was in his tent and he was very pleased to see me – particularly because the route up to the Regiment that evening was difficult and an Officer was required to travel with each Regimental group of lorries. He didn't want to have to go himself so my arrival was a blessing.

He fed me and we set off. The drill was to follow the Divisional Markers which were a sheet metal oval set on a metal post. These were sited at a suitable frequency for drivers to follow in bad light. If you couldn't see the next marker you had to stop, get out and lie on the ground to see if you could see it silhouetted against the night sky. There were minefields all around and just after the first light we passed the remains of one of our

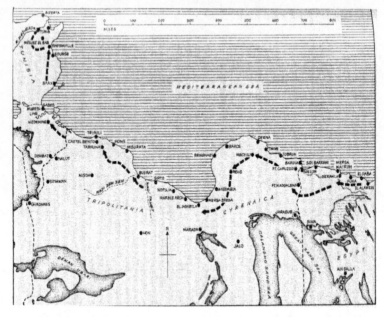

The progress of 7th Armoured Division in North Africa, 1942-43

Sketch of My Truck . SURI

83

Regiment's vehicles which I knew to be that of a man I had been to school with and I feared the worst. He had in fact been killed. Eventually we reached the Regiment and I reported for duty – it was early December 1942.

The man who had been blown up in that mine was Gavin Nicholson who had been Captain of the School at Glenalmond in my second year, so he was three or four years senior to me and was already in G Battery when I joined the Regiment in October 1941. It is interesting after all these years to recall how one reacts at the time to these deaths of men who were your friends. Although the first reaction was obviously one of great sadness you could not allow yourself to become too deeply affected and you tended to put a ring around your emotions – a sort of hardness of heart – because the battle had to go on and you had to play your part. Since this sort of warfare went on in my case for nearly three years I have no doubt that I learned to keep emotions strictly under control and though this was helpful at the time it was not easy to give them free rein after the war was over. I am sure this must have been other people's experience also.

6

Tripoli

"Yet rightly pitch my moving tent
A day's march nearer home"
James Montgomery.

During my absence the 8th Armoured Division had been disbanded and the Regiments allocated to other existing divisions, so 5RHA were now part of the 7th Armoured Division – the Desert Rats, with whom we served for the rest of the war. The Divisional Commander was General John Harding (later Lord Harding of the Petherton – Field Marshal). I was immediately appointed Regimental Survey Officer, succeeding Paddy Victory who went across to K Battery.

The terrain we were in was stony desert. There was the one coastal road, not always very close to the coast, and that was all. So we spent our time finding our way across featureless desert, normally fairly flat and stony but with patches of soft sand that we did our best to avoid. Quite frequently we encountered wadis, which are dried riverbeds; some of these were very small and hardly noticeable and others were deep and wide and presented an obstacle. Sometimes it became very stony and we bounced for miles over rocks the size of footballs.

The basic unit for everyone was their vehicle, and mine was an 8cwt truck with an enclosed cab for driver and passenger and a hole in the cab roof for the passenger – me – to stand up and use the sun compass on the roof above the driver. The back of the truck had a canvas tilt on a tubular frame and was open at the back. It was a rear wheel drive vehicle and we had sand channels carried on either side, which were much used. If one stuck on soft sand the drill was for everyone to get out and using shovels dig the sand away from the front of the rear wheels and lay the sand channels so that they were immediately in front of these wheels. Then we all pushed, picked up the shovels and sand channels and pursued the truck until it either stuck again or was able to stop on firm ground. It was quite exhausting and also dangerous if there were enemy aircraft about.

In my case there was the driver and either two or three surveyors in the back with our instruments etc. They used to suffer from the dust because as the truck travelled along a dusty track the suction would pull the dust into the truck and after a journey the men would emerge looking like snowmen.

I remember two of the men in my truck at that time. One was Bdr Edwards whose civilian career was to be art work for the advertising world. He subsequently got a commission and I met him once after the war looking very prosperous. And the other was Bdr Timms whom I have seen once or twice at regimental reunions with his son who looks now exactly the same as his father did then. Also R Selfe whom I have seen since and Gunner Wharton – a Yorkshire postman.

We did a bit of experimental cooking to enliven the rather monotonous diet. One recipe was to put some of the hard biscuits into a bag and hit them with a hammer against the side of the truck until they were pulverised and then moisten them with water and cook it like a suet pudding with jam. All we could say about it is that it was different!

We were kept up to date with world news by the arrival of the Army Newspaper every few days. Amongst other things this had the regular cartoon of the Two Types who were outrageous RAF officers with huge handlebar moustaches and equally outrageous jokes. They provided light relief. The Regimental paperwork was handled by the Adjutant's office truck with its lean to canvas extension and worn out typewriters infiltrated with sand. How they kept their papers in order, I don't know. They were mainly dealing with Base Headquarters known as 2nd Echelon where the office in charge was O2E. On the canvas of the office truck was pinned the ditty:

With reference yours from O2E
oblique stroke H oblique stroke 3
oblique stroke K oblique stroke 8
A few more strokes and then the date
Here is the cry for which you yearn
Another bloody nil return

I had two roles. As soon as the guns moved their positions – and in this campaign it was always forward – I and my team had to swing into action and survey them into their new positions. This had to be done as quickly as possible but it often took an hour or two. When this had been done I was available to do other things and more often than not this involved acting as Personal Assistant to Colonel Gregson. He used to move around not only to our Batteries but also to the tank or infantry regiments which we were supporting. As a result he was often as well informed about the situation as anyone in the Division, and the Divisional Commander (Major General) would be keen to talk to him whenever they met. For me it was all intensely interesting.

One of the problems of warfare is that it is very difficult to know what is going on. You do your job, you fire and get fired on but you do not know whether things are going well or badly. During these visits that I made with Peter Gregson we would meet the Commanders of other formations in the Division and find out what was happening in their particular part of the action. It was a two-way traffic because we could pass on information we had learnt from others.

When we were in action, which was most of the time, rations were distributed to each vehicle and the driver was normally the cook. The method of heating water either for tea or for cooking was to use a brew can. Both water and petrol at that time were delivered in "flimsies". These were very unsatisfactory metal containers about 12" square and 18" tall. The metal was too thin and they frequently punctured, but they were all we had until the Army copied the German jerry can.

The brew can was cut out of a "flimsy" and was then 12" square, about 6" high with holes knocked through the sides about 4" up. This was half filled with sand and, say, two pints of petrol poured into the sand; a match was thrown in and the pan put on the top. It was quite effective and when you were finished with it you just emptied it on to the ground and hung it to your towing hook.

Our ration was one gallon of water per day for all purposes. We used about a pint of this for washing and shaving, some for cooking and the rest we drank as tea. We drank none of it as water since in those conditions warm water does not quench your thirst as well as tea. The food was hard biscuits (no bread), margarine, jam, meat and vegetable stew (M & V), bully beef and occasionally tinned bacon and Soya links (sausage made from Soya flour). There was no fruit and no green vegetables but we took Ascorbic Acid tablets to guard against scurvy and later Mepacrine tablets against malaria.

Your "luggage" consisted of a haversack with your toothbrush and razor and other small items and also your bedding roll into which you packed your spare clothes, pyjamas (if ever you wore them) and anything else. In my case I had a lilo in the bedding roll so that I didn't feel any of the stones underneath me. If it was cold or windy we each had a "bivvy" (small one man tent) to sleep in; if there was a risk of enemy shellfire we each dug a small trench and slept in that. I made myself get up in the morning by pulling the plugs of my lilo! We used to go to bed soon after it was pitch dark and get up an hour before first light.

Washing ourselves and washing clothes was more of a problem. The normal procedure was that when we had a day when we were not likely to move or be active the message would go round that the water truck would make a special visit and give us enough water to wash ourselves and our clothes. Drying them was not normally a problem. My recollection of thease days, 60 years on, is that we coped remarkably well with the problems of life. Letters from home were very important and came through fairly regularly. Health was good apart from "Desert Sores" which were small ulcers on hands and legs, which wouldn't heal. Probably caused by our diet of no fresh food. Morale was excellent because we were always moving forward and we knew that we were having a good "press" at home.

If we were likely to be stopped for more than a couple of days which happened only occasionally – for instance at Christmas - then rations would not be distributed to trucks but instead separate messes would be established for Other Ranks, Sergeants/Warrant Officers and Officers.

Food would be cooked at each of these messes. This is certainly what happened for a few days over Christmas 1942. On this occasion some special food and drink was sent up and we had a good celebration. I remember the CO2 saying "We have plenty of whisky but go easy on the water". I think there were about ten of us in RHQ Officers' Mess, so it was quite a small party.

There was one difficulty in this arrangement and that was getting back to bed. Because we did not want to present a target to enemy aircraft each of our trucks had to be at least one hundred yards away from its neighbour and this could mean that you had a five hundred yard walk to the mess tent. It was daylight when you left so you took a compass bearing, memorized it and then carefully counted the number of paces to the tent. When you emerged after dinner it was pitch dark, so you set your compass on your back-bearing and began to count the number of paces. You were not always exactly on target and if you couldn't see your truck you lay on the ground to get it silhouetted against what light there was It wasn't very easy and there were occasions when people spent a lot of the night finding their way home!

A few days before Christmas we reached the border between Cyrenaica and Tripolitania, which was marked by a huge triumphal arch erected by Mussolini to mark the border of his newly acquired territory. This was known to us as "Marble Arch". Not far beyond it was a large wadi, which became the separation between us and the enemy over the four days of Christmas when there was little or no hostile activity on either side.

On the afternoon of Christmas Day 1942 we had a football match between the Officers' and the Sergeants' messes. The game was made more difficult by the existence of ant heaps every few yards. There was a handicap system by which, whenever a goal was scored, the winning side had to drink a tot of gin. This had the effect of evening out the advantages and the game came to a natural end after a few goals had been scored.

On the next day the CO, Rawdon Hoare, told me to accompany him to reconnoitre a route through the wadi in front of us. We set off in two jeeps. I was in front with my driver and he behind us. We found a suitable route without much difficulty and the enemy did not disturb us. On the way back to the Regiment – probably four or five miles – we were crossing a stretch of empty nothingness when suddenly all hell was let loose and we realized that we were being machine-gunned by enemy fighter aircraft. It was over in a few seconds and when we came to a halt I shouted to everyone to leave their jeeps in case the aircraft came round again. I was glad to see that all four of us were still mobile. We had run off only a few yards when the planes reappeared and as they attacked the jeeps we lay spread-eagled on the open ground. I have never felt so naked and helpless. After the second attack they flew off and we went back to pick up the pieces. Miraculously three of us were unhurt and only the CO had been hit. He wasn't too bad and was able to walk. His jeep was out of action but mine was all right except for its brakes, which were inoperative. We took him in tow and when we got back to the Regiment the CO was evacuated. He made a complete recovery, but we did not see him again. His successor, who arrived a few days later, was Peter Gregson who Commanded for the next eighteen months and for whom I had the greatest respect.

Rawdon Hoare had been a very good training commander but he was not sufficiently outgoing to inspire troops in action. He was very particular about his dress and appearance – and there was a suspicion of scent! You could never relax in his presence –

he was a Roman Catholic and insisted on having his own priest at hand so the Regiment unusually had two Padres-one C of E and one RC. The former was an Irishman called Synott and a veteran of the first world war. The RC man was Rice - nicknamed Pudding of course. I was told that Rawdon had a special relationship with a man at the war office and insisted on choosing which officers would be appointed to 5RHA. So, in a way, we were all handpicked! We all respected him but not many of us liked him.

Our new CO Peter Gregson was a regular soldier and a very keen horseman, very outgoing and with a wonderful sense of humour. He was the complete antithesis of his predecessor and very easy to talk to. He had been commanding a Battery of guns in the Eritrea campaign and I remember him telling me of one occasion when he and his signaller had climbed to the top of a mountain or hill in order to get observation of the enemy and direct the fire of his guns. Unfortunately he was seen by an Italian aircraft who proceeded to attack him. There was no cover on the hilltop except one large tree. So Peter and his signaller stood one side of the tree when the aircraft attacked from the other side and vice-versa until the Italian gave up.

Soon after Christmas we continued our pressure westward. The normal procedure at this time was for the enemy to hold us up on a particular line with his guns and tanks. We would attack them during the day and they would withdraw during the night to avoid being encircled from the south. His object was to achieve an orderly withdrawal. By mid-January we paused for supplies to catch up with us and now we received one of Monty's printed messages for all the troops. Instead of the usual secrecy he gave us all the information about our own forces and those of the enemy and told us that we were now going to make for Tripoli on two fronts. The Highland Division and others would attack up the coast road through Misurata and we – and others – would go out into the desert and attack Tripoli from the south. He said that we had supplies for a week and would have to capture Tripoli in that time or go hungry!

So we set off and after traversing some very difficult terrain were being attacked by Stukas. It was fortunate and mainly thanks to the Desert Air Force that these attacks did not happen more frequently. When they came for you it was important to keep moving and weave about a bit like a ship at sea avoiding torpedoes. The Germans had fitted sirens to the wings of their Stuka Dive Bombers so that as they dived at you they emitted a shriek, which added to the tension. The worst thing was to be stuck in the sand when they attacked. We lost a few vehicles and a few lives but not very many.

We came at Tarhuna to the range of hills, which mark the southern limit of the more fertile Tripoli region. The enemy had some heavy guns here and we had to approach in open formation with vehicles well separated from each other over an open plain. It was more like naval warfare than a land operation. It wasn't enjoyable but very few of their shells did any damage and we closed up to the pass into the mountains just as darkness fell. The only reaction that I can remember is that both my driver and I reached for our steel helmets and put them on our heads. This is the only time I remember wearing it. An excerpt from my letter of 21st refers to this:

> *".. We didn't have any difficult at wadi Zem Zem – he just didn't seem inclined to stay! We had just a little the day before though when we pushed across the Bungem road. The real surprise though of the whole battle was the ease with which we got into the hills at Tarhuna. The natural defences are enormous since the Southerly wind blowing up against the*

high hills which form a barrier around Tripoli have created a huge barrier of soft sand which is quite impassable except along the one track. I think he probably didn't like his left flank on the coast ...

At the moment we are a lot further west than we were on Jan 17th. We have had some interesting days and some appallingly bumpy going. The country now is much more like the country you imagine when you read Beau Geste with sweating soldiers of the Foreign Legion living and dying and saying odd things!

The news at the moment is good in most places but the Americans seem to have caught a packet in Tunisia. It is a pity they had to go back because it is going to make it so much more difficult for us but we will get over all difficulties. I think it needs the 8th Army to clear up things in

Tunisia; so don't worry! Jerry will be out
of Africa by the middle of May at the
latest.

From there our motorized infantry cleared minor enemy resistance and we drove through the night to reach Tripoli early in the morning of 23rd January – and five hours ahead of the Highlanders.

My letter home was five days later and dated 28 January 1943.

Dear Everyone,

I wrote you rather a hurried airgraph the
day before yesterday first to keep you
going, but I said very little in it; I will be
more detailed now because I don't think it
can do any harm. You heard no doubt on
the news about the capture of Tripoli;
well we were in the force that came up
from the desert and reached it first. We
had quite a good battle and it really was

103

a pleasure to reach the city the 8th army has been trying to reach for years. We moved fast as I expect you gathered. We were covering about 50 miles a day across smooth hard sand, across stony boulder strewn plateaus, across deep wadis, along the soft beds of wadis and finally along the straight and narrow road. I was still doing my job of survey officer and used to swanning around sticking poles in here and there. My truck is an 8 cwt, which is the usual form of a cab for driver and passenger, and the canvas-covered body behind which will seat two; actually there are only 3 of us on it altogether. They are very good and quite fast but it didn't like the big stones and boulders we went over all one day. We carried water and food and petrol to last us days and days and were quite self-

supportive. We used to get up at about 0630, move off at 0800 having had no breakfast since it was too dark to light fires, have our breakfast at the first halt which may not have been till eleven o'clock, have something to eat if we could at 1 o'clock and then have our evening meal at the first opportunity after 5 o'clock. Sometimes it was dark before we had a chance and our meal had to be cold. We were usually in bed by 9 o'clock. It was a great change when we got into the more fertile parts nearer Tripoli when we could refill our water cans and the ground had some grass growing on it. It wasn't a hard battle and the RAF supported us very well, but to begin with we used to have a regular shuttle service of Stukas coming over and hotting us up. They are not pleasant but if you are in a slit trench and just below ground level you feel a terrific confidence that nothing can touch you and, what is more, you are just about right since there is nothing to fall on you as there is when a town is bombed. We didn't do more than go into the outskirts of Tripoli ourselves since the Hun had to be pushed back a reasonable distance from Tripoli and his ideas of 'reasonable' and ours don't quite agree! So the great work goes on; and when you consider the distance we are from our base at Cairo, you must admit that it is a great work; I don't know how far it is from Cairo to Tripoli but it must be within 200 miles of the 2000 mark. We are in a much more English sort of climate at the moment; it is overcast and drizzling with rain. The coastal area is a chain of little oases spreading out from the big one of

Tripoli; they are usually covered with palm trees and lived in by Arabs who do a bit of cultivation on a small scale. On the outskirts are Italian houses (and some oases consist of a complete and new Italian village) with wind pumps and gardens and considerable produce. We are living on fresh cabbage, potatoes and carrots at the moment, not to mention eggs and, on one occasion a chicken! We also managed to get hold of some local wine, a sort of Chianti, and it was very good. Apart from odd patches of property the country is very poor and bare. The Germans fleeced it when they were there and when we were coming up the Italians left and the Arabs pillaged all the farms. It is only with the greatest difficulty that we manage to get anything at all; but all things considered we feed very well; we

107

still miss bread and potatoes and fresh meat.

I had a most nerve-racking experience the other day; everything was very fluid and I was spinning around at night looking for a particular unit. I was going along a narrow lane, which I didn't know to be definitely clear and I saw something looming up ahead. I was straining my eyes to see what it was (I was by myself in a jeep) when suddenly there was a roar on either side and a couple of hounds leapt at me barking loudly and just then the object turned out to be a tank obstruction with a narrow pass through it. I nearly jumped out of my seat but I was soon the other side of the obstruction unscathed!

We passed through Tripoli and were directed to stop west of the town and right by the edge of the sea. I was feeling hot and dirty after a week of continuous activity so decided to have a swim. I cut the barbed wire with wire-cutters and carefully walking only on stones in case there were mines I stepped into the water, which was surprisingly cold but very refreshing. I was then looking forward to at least a day of leisure but very soon we were told to move on within the hour. It was decided that we must keep the pressure up but we were so short of supplies - until Tripoli harbour could be opened up - that the Army advance consisted only of one Brigade, which was ours.

Progress was slow because the road passed through some swampy land and with the road blown the tanks could not get across so everything had to stop until the Engineers could build a new causeway. One night we had one Battery isolated on the other side of a blown bridge and running out of ammunition. There was a railway line which offered a possible route forward and I was ordered to take three 3 ton lorries with ammunition and try to reach them. I took the lorries back to the nearest station where we could get on to the track and with one pair of wheels between the lines and one to the right of them we bounced forward. Inevitably we met a truck coming the other way; we could clear each other at ground level but the tops of the canopies would not clear. So we had men sitting on top of the canopies pushing the opposite canopy away as we gradually passed each other. We eventually reached our destination. They were very glad to see us because the enemy were in front of them and they were very low in ammunition.

By the middle of February we were approaching the Mareth Line – a fortified zone built by the French to defend their territory from the east. In order to close up to it we had to cross an open plain with the enemy in possession of the hills at the other side of it and able to bring their guns to bear on us as we crossed. The plan was to cross this plain at first light – well spaced out – and with all non-essential vehicles left behind. To our great relief the morning started with a thick mist and we raced across the ground in order to reach the other side before the mist lifted and our tanks, in a very spirited attack, cleared the enemy from the hill – subsequently known as Edinburgh Castle.

7

Triumph in Tunis

*"Here is my journey's end, here is my butt
And very sea mark of my utmost sail
Shakespeare.*

The Brigade had now reached a stage where for several reasons it had to pause. The first reason was that we were very thin on the ground and our supply lines were very long. As we went west our lines became longer and Rommel's became shorter. Additionally Rommel had a number of divisions under his command in Tunisia which could easily overwhelm us if we became over-extended. A further point is that we had reached the Mareth line which was a relatively easy place for the enemy to defend It was now 20th February and the Highland Division came up on the following day and held the line between Medenine and the sea. Basically the 'Mareth line' was a defensive position which had been prepared to repel attacks from the East. It was not a complicated series of structures and tunnels like the French Maginot line but had been fully surveyed and prepared with tank ditches, pill boxes and gun emplacements. By using these facilities the enemy could resist attack with relatively few troops.

In a further message to the troops Monty said that he expected a German counter-attack on 6th March and spelt out for us exactly what formations would join us and when – including the important information that the new 17 pounder anti-tank gun would be ready for action, which I and many others went to inspect as soon as it arrived. The importance of this gun cannot be over-emphasized. For all of the past two years in the desert we had been out-gunned by the Germans who had the 88mm, which could knock out any of our tanks at quite a long range. We had nothing to equal it. Our tanks had first a 2 pdr, then a 6 pdr and then a 75mm gun, but these could only knock out a German tank at fairly close quarters. I have never understood why the Army did not convert our 3.7 anti-aircraft guns to a ground role and give us an effective answer to the 88mm. However the 17 pounder was what we wanted but we had only a handful of them.

At the time I wondered how it was that Monty was so certain that we would be attacked on 6th March and it is only in the last few years that I have realized that it was the result of code breaking of Enigma at Bletchley Park. Monty was quite right and the Germans put in their attack on schedule but as we were ready for them and not off-balance we saw them off and lost no ground with only a few casualties. Soon after, however, the 201 Guards Brigade put in an attack on the Horseshoe Feature and though they reached their objective, they were cut off and lost a number of men in making their way back.

The Battle of Mareth started in earnest on 21st March and only limited progress was made in the frontal attacks. Monty then sent a column of tanks with New Zealand Infantry on board around the left flank at El

Hamma and turned the enemy's position so that he was forced to retreat. Then we all moved forward to the next enemy position on the Wadi Akarit.

Another frontal attack was needed to force our way across this feature and it is interesting to read in the Divisional history that 7th Armoured Division were not involved in the attack on Wadi Akarit and that this was the first time they had been out of contact with the enemy since Alamein five months before. We, as Divisional Artillery, however, were involved and played our part in the attack, which was immediately successful.

Our role as a regiment was to bring our guns into action as close up as possible to the wadi without being exposed to view and then as the attack progressed to move our guns forward in order to support the infantry and tanks. The enemy's job was, among other things, to find out where we were and to shell us. My role was to find out where our Batteries were going to site their guns or where they had already done so and to survey them in so that they could all shoot together and with accuracy.

It was at about this time that I wrote home.

8/3/43

Dear Mother and Father,

A most unfortunate thing has happened. I wrote a masterly letter to you in reply to an air letter card of Father's and I am blessed if the thing hasn't gone up in smoke and little pieces with a truck, so I will have to do it all over again. Before I start I must tell you a story that made me laugh like a drain: A "base-wallah" (you know the kind of chap I mean) got fed up with all the taunts and jibes people were casting at him and asked for permission to go on a little private commando raid; his wish was granted and he was given a camel and some necessary equipment and off he went. Nothing was heard of him for some 3 weeks till all of a sudden a message appeared, reading "Rommel captured, am returning home". Terrific jubilation, his name at once became well known and his feat appraised. About 3 days later however another message arrived reading "cancel last message, should read – Camel ruptured, am walking home"!! So much for that.

Now as far as general conditions are concerned, I am absolutely as fit as a fiddle and getting enough to eat; up till now I have considered that as assumed, and have not mentioned it. I haven't had any health troubles since I have been out here. We are parked at the moment in a field of barley, it is 2 o'clock and the sun is really hot. I am sitting in my shirtsleeves by my truck. Round about

117

there are scores of beautiful flowers among the barley. There are purple pimpernels, arabis white and arabis yellow, cornflowers, poppies, orchids, daisies, dandelions and yellow mustard. The barley is in ear but not ripe. It is about 18" high. We are having some rain, in fact it poured with rain the night before last, but it usually confines its activities to the night very conveniently.

The contours of the land are quite pleasant. It is an open plain broken by wadis and gullies and a little undulating. The surface is hard sand with gravel and little scrub on it where the Arabs haven't ploughed and sown it; there are plenty of wells. Rising out of the plain is a high block of hills that dominates it, and they are connected by a rough and rather broad neck to the higher hills behind.

Palm trees abound and odd little thatched wooden huts built by and for the Arabs; there are also stone buildings and mosques scattered about; all buildings are untouchable; they smell and are infected with lice and vermin.

We had a little battle the other day; the foolish Hun misjudged his man and we gave him a "bloody nose" (in the exact words of Montgomery's instructions!); I think he will think twice before he tries again!!

I had a letter from Colin Lyall the other day; he is out here and I would like to see him again. I answered his letter and that will have to be rewritten too! He is in a Depot at the moment waiting to be posted. All these places seem such miles away and that, of course is exactly what they are!!

Someone went into Tripoli the other day and brought back a live pig amongst other things; we are going to fatten it up and let it grow till it will grow no more and kill for a thanks-offering at Bizerta; it ought to be quite tasty then; I wonder what else we can rake up?

Well, I reckon the war is going well; it seems so ingrained in one now that it would be quite unbelievable if it came to an end this year; in fact it coming to an end at all seems something of a dream, and yet it is <u>not</u> so much of a dream as one imagines. I wonder where we go from Tunis?

My love to all,

Andrew

P.S.   Somebody lost my knife for me, curse them.

120

Colin Lyall was a school friend.

Just as we were all pouring across the wadi in pursuit I had to go back and collect my survey poles and in the process got separated from my Regiment and was quite unable to locate them when it started to become dark; so we dossed down for the night and next morning we set off again and I saw in the distance the easily recognizable ACV's of Brigade HQ and I called in to ask where 5 RHA were! Fortunately I was given an accurate answer by Brian Wyldbore-Smith and was relieved to be back a short time later. My vehicle was not equipped with a wireless set.

We then made rapid progress north through Southern Tunisia and came fairly close to the holy city of Kairouan, which we were told not to shell. Our vehicles by this time were getting fairly worn out and we captured one or two Italian lorries, which were a great help. One of them was a large Field Lorry with an inertia starter, which we had not seen before. It had no battery and its starting handle did not turn the engine directly, but built up speed on a heavy flywheel. To start the truck you turned this wheel faster and faster and then pulled a cord which transferred its energy to the engine and with luck it started.

There was something of a pause at this moment and my next letter has more to say about the countryside.

13 April 1943

Dear Mother and Father,

I have had a few letters from you but I think it is more important to give you an idea of what is happening here than making many comments on communicated facts. Thank you both very much for your letters nevertheless. I enjoy getting them a lot.

I think I last wrote to you on April 6th. Great things have happened since then. We fought the enemy on the Akarit line and gave him a terrific thrashing. He left

122

everything and went running home lickety spit. You cannot imagine the amount of stuff of every kind and shape that he left behind, and when I say "stuff" I include Italians. They came flocking in in thousands, driving their own cars, carrying their own cases. Literally, with no escort at all, looking more like tramps than anything else. We came through innumerable minefields and I was out in a Jeep and got separated from my H.Q. on a job. I couldn't find them again when I got back since they were moving on so fast and I spent the rest of the day looking for them. I hadn't found them by night so I cadged a meal and joined them early next morning. A rather unfortunate little episode but it turned out all O.K.

Since then we have been plodding along up to Sfax. We made quite good progress the first day, better the second, still better the third, till eventually we were doing up to 50 miles a day. Since we got out of the Gabes plain we came into a country that was bristling with olive groves. It is undulating land and in places you can look for miles and miles and see nothing but olive groves arranged in neat rows, with the ground in between ploughed, which makes very heavy going in a car. Unfortunately the olives aren't ripe yet, they are not even formed.

We bypassed Sfax in exactly the same way as we did Tripoli and so I haven't been into either yet. Water is of course abundant, so one doesn't go thirsty, which is an absolute Godsend. I loathe being thirsty!

Today I had a very interesting trip. We went up a road a certain distance through

124

beds of flowers that were beautiful beyond all imagination. They were carpeted in all colours of the rainbow for miles and miles. I wished I had a colour film. Later we left the main road and went across a little road through the plain till we hit a bridge that was a little rickety and impassable so we made a detour and crossed over a bridge that was still rickety but just passable. Then after passing through marshes and trees we got back into another and arrived where we wanted. I thoroughly enjoyed the trip. We finished up near a little station with wind pump, well, waiting room and ticket office all absolutely deserted, but rather pleasantly situated amongst the trees.

Will write again tomorrow to finish my rambles.

Much love,

Andrew

We now closed up to the area of Enfidaville and were faced with a range of mountains held by the Germans who, as a result, controlled the flat land to the south and towards the sea in the east. The Ghurkhas of 4th Indian Division made a gallant attack up the steep cliff by night with their Kukris and, not surprisingly, the Germans fled.

One of the things I remember most clearly is the way the 8th Army contained divisions from so many different countries from what we knew at that time as the Empire. Fighting alongside us were the 2nd New Zealand Division and the 4th Indian Division. The Australians had been with us but were withdrawn to their home country to resist a possible attack by the Japanese. The South African Division had also been active earlier on. In addition to these we were joined at Mareth by the Free French Brigade under General Leclerc who had come up from West Africa, crossing the desert to come under command of 8th Army and for much of the time part of the 7th Armoured Division. I didn't come across these troops personally although I saw their Brigade signs on vehicles and road markers. What we did not have was troops from the United States or Canada until we met them at Tunis coming up from the west with 1st Army.

Extract from letter 16/4/43 – S.Tunisia.

"We are still very much on the job and I think I would not like to be Jerry very much at the moment. He is about to pay for his sins and he knows it. We will soonhave him screaming for mercy and I don't think he will get an awful lot.We have been moving about a bit and I have had some marvellous views. The sun and shadow over the hills is sometimes amazingly fine. When there is a lot of small clouds in the sky the whole landscape is speckled shadow

We are doing a little bargaining up here. One shirt gets you a hen or 10 eggs and if you are lucky a sheep

127

for 2 shirts. I had a bit of lamb tonight with some fresh French beans of which there are stacks.

It is a very nice country really with flocks of sheep and herds of cows, goats mules and some jolly fine horses. This part of the world is of course famous for its pure breed of horses, Sand is turning into clay"

The first plan was for us to leave our non-essential vehicles behind and force our way up the coastal plain under the guns of the enemy on the high ground to our left. This would have been a dangerous operation and fortunately it was changed to plan two. On 30th April the Division moved west into the desert and then north to join 1st Army in North Tunisia who were trying to attack Tunis from the west. This was a fascinating journey; we moved away from the more fertile areas into uninhabited territory with occasional Roman remains and then, after turning north, we came into country with trees again and cultivated ground. Our route took us through Maktar and Le Krib.

We were astonished when we joined the 1st Army. Whereas our trucks were yellow, theirs' were green and they were all dutifully screened with camouflage nets, which we used only infrequently because we had been involved in a war of movement.

We arrived in the area of Medjez-el-Bab on 2nd May 1943, my 21st birthday. The CO Peter Gregson knew this and, having a few hours to spare, said he would like to go and see his brother Martin Gregson at Army Group HQ which was about twenty miles away and I was to come too. So the two of us went off in a jeep and found the HQ in 1st Army area and Peter's brother. After an hour or so we drove back. It was then getting dark and we were getting hungry. We passed through a small Tunisian town where we saw the sign for a Restaurant so we stopped and entered only to find that it was occupied by an American staff officer. He regretted that the Restaurant was closed but said that he would be 'tickled pink' if we were to stay and have a meal with him. We said that, of course, we wouldn't think of putting him to this trouble and went off to find somewhere else. There was, of course, nowhere else and Peter said let us go back and "tickle that American pink" – so we did! We got back to the Regiment rather late.

Bearing in mind that we were about to launch a major attack on the enemy three days later this all seems very light hearted and not concentrating on the job in hand, but that is the way it was. The CO had issued his orders and was free to go where he wanted and my absence didn't affect anyone. It was a delightful way to celebrate a birthday!

Meanwhile the Division lined up alongside 4th Indian Division (our old friends) on our left and 6th Armoured Division (1st Army) on our right.

In an astonishingly short time of three days we launched a powerful attack towards Tunis. It was hilly country and we took the 'highroad' and 6th Armoured Division took the 'low road' and we strove to reach Tunis before them. Our advance was fiercely resisted all the way as evidenced by the burnt out enemy tanks we passed and it was the second day before we reached the crest of the hill and looked down on the city several hundred feet below us. As the tanks first and we behind them began the descent, it started to rain and we then knew that nothing would stop us from capturing the town we had come all this way to occupy (some 1800 miles). It has always been a matter of debate whether our 11th Hussars or the 1st Army's 2nd Derbyshire Yeomanry were the first to enter Tunis. It was a close run thing and in the end didn't really matter, but pride in one's own formation has always been a powerful spur to achievement. We stopped just outside the town and were not involved in any further action though other parts of the Division and of the Army had more to do to clear up enemy resistance in the Cape Bon Peninsula and elsewhere.

On that first evening two of us thought we would go into Tunis and see what it looked like, so we took a jeep and drove into the centre where everything was very quiet. It was dark and there were no streetlights but we saw a lantern outside what was clearly an hotel. We went in and found one or two people having a drink so we ordered one for ourselves. Suddenly a series of shots rang out and the manager ran to us and said one of our soldiers was shooting at his guests. When we investigated we found a British Signals Dispatch rider who had obviously had too much to drink waving his revolver around. It isn't difficult for two sober people to disarm one drunk one, so we took his revolver and threw him out.

The next morning word came to me from somewhere that the German equivalent of the NAAFI was in a certain street and worth investigating. I got the CO's permission and with three soldiers took the big Italian truck and found the store. We broke in and entered a real Aladdin's Cave with food, drink and other stores which we had been short of for so long. Since this was a military store we had no compunction in taking what we wanted and so we began to load the lorry with crates of this and that. But we were surrounded by a crowd of very hungry Tunisians who took off the lorry everything we put on. A change of plan was needed. I recruited three men from the crowd and with a promise to pay them in kind I put them to work carrying the crates and put my three soldiers with their rifles on the lorry to keep the crowd at bay. On my return to the Regiment I asked the CO how to dispose of my loot and he told me to put a low price on everything and to sell it. Since the troops had not had anything to spend their money on for six months they would have no hesitation in buying what they wanted – mainly food items such as tinned fruit etc. We did this under the Sergeant Major's control and Battery and RHQ profited with an input to their funds, which came in very useful later on. One of the items was cases of Kummel – a powerful cumin flavoured liqueur made in North Germany. This was distributed to each of the Officer's Messes and provided a pre-dinner drink for the next few months.

On the following day we were watching the roads as the streams of dejected prisoners were marching in. As they came by I noticed two men in the German equivalent of a jeep, which I immediately coveted, so I stopped the vehicle and told them to get out and walk. They said they were Generals and should be allowed to drive, but we turned them out nevertheless and made them walk. Their vehicle came in very useful.

I will always look back on these few days as one of the highpoints of my life. The exhilaration of reaching one's objective and taking a quarter of a million enemy prisoners was immense. It was really a major German setback and closely followed the German defeat at Stalingrad.

Although the 8th Army went on to capture Sicily and then crossed over into Italy and fought up the Adriatic Coast until the war ended, Tunis marked the end of the distinctive 8th Army. Afterwards it was much like any other Army, but before Tunis it had a character all its own. With its penchant for strange and gaudy clothes worn by many of the officers when they ought to have been in uniform, the frequent use of Arabic words as slang, the supreme self-confidence and openness, the feeling that their unusual experiences with a mixture of ups and downs had made them different from anyone else and their pride – all this tended to fade when the next Campaign in Sicily and Italy started a few months later. But everyone who was a member of that army was forever after proud to have been so.

The Campaign that had just finished had been dominated by the characters of two men – Montgomery and Rommel. Montgomery was a very unusual man – very conceited and self-centred – not clubbable in any way but a real professional as a soldier who had studied the art of war. He must have been a very awkward man to have under one's command and both Alexander and Eisenhower must have had limitless patience and forbearance. But to those of us who served under him he was a hero and we would have followed him to the ends of the earth. He knew exactly how to relate to his troops and he always told them everything he could. He planned well ahead and because things tended to happen in the way he predicted, we came to believe his promises and forecasts.

We only knew Rommel by his actions. He fought a brilliant rearguard action all the way from Egypt to Tunis and was never caught seriously off balance. His German troops were dogged and dangerous and we had a healthy respect for them. At no stage was our advance a walkover. The Italians, by contrast, were a joke. We once overran an Italian formation and in their 2nd echelon found a large and well-furnished vehicle marked 'Fornicatorium Mobile'. History does not relate whether with or without staff!

There was also an element of chivalry. We never came across mass murders but there was only a sparse population in the desert and they were only ever marginally involved. We would look after the enemy wounded and they would do the same for ours. As an example there was the famous occasion in May 1942 (before we came on the scene) when 7th Armoured Division Commander Major General Messervy was captured along with several of his HQ officers. As soon as he was taken prisoner he took off all his badges of rank and appeared before his captors with no rank. When asked why a man of his apparent age should be fighting a young man's war he replied that there was always a need for someone to clean the latrines. He was put with the 'other ranks' and escaped that night and returned to command his Division.

Except possibly for the concentration of forces for the Battle of Alamein, the 8th Army was always relatively small and there were never more than two Corps Commanders (of whom Lt-Gen Brian Horrocks was the best known and most respected). As a result we pretended to know who everyone was and each Division had its reputation and respect. We had confidence in our senior officers up to and very much including Montgomery and with all these factors in our favour it is not surprising that the 8th Army became a superb fighting force and that the Germans chose, in the end, to surrender to Montgomery and to no-one else.

Up to 19th January our Divisional Commander had been General Harding but on this day, on our way to Tripoli, we had stopped for the night on a stony hilltop and we happened to be very close to Adv. Division HQ It was always a problem to know when you were going to be on the move so as not to be caught with a half-brewed mug of tea and I remember saying to my driver that we were all right because we wouldn't be moving until the General came back from his short walk with his shovel over his shoulder. When he did this and climbed onto the Brigade Commander's tank a bombardment of enemy shells came down on us. Harding was blown off his tank on to the ground. His injuries were not life threatening but he had to be evacuated and hand over command of the division. Brigadier Pip Roberts, who later commanded 11th Armoured Division, took over temporarily until Major General Bobby Erskine was appointed.

It was at about this time that I was involved in a life saving operation for one of our Troop Commanders. Alan Burrough was one of our FOOs operating with the tanks in an attack on an enemy position which went sadly wrong. Alan's tank was knocked out early in the day along with a number of our other tanks and the enemy remained in control of the battlefield. It was not possible to rescue any wounded because of this and we did not know whether or not Alan and his crew had survived. At about 9pm when it was quite dark and we had all dossed down for the night, I was woken with a message that the Tank Regiment had recovered Alan who was seriously injured but alive. He had lain for the whole of that day in his shattered tank alongside his crew or their bodies. I organised my crew and we set off in the complete dark with, of course, no vehicle lights. There were no tracks so we had to find our way by bearing to where the Tank Regiment were. We eventually did this and picked up a sedated Alan and then had to find our way to the RAMC. It was a difficult journey not only from a navigational point of view but also because you couldn't see what sort of ground you were passing and we went over a ridge of only about six inches but it felt, for a moment, like a cliff. Eventually we delivered Alan to the care of the medics and though he lost half of one leg he went to live a full life and nearly won the Goblet Sculls at Henley Regatta with only 1½ legs in 1947!

My letter of 17 May 1943 gives an idea of the sense of elation we all felt.

> *Dear Mother and Father,*
>
> *I am now going to start, and hope to complete, the promised letter in which I am going to explain the happenings of the last few weeks, for I have indeed a lot of leeway to make up, and it hasn't been an uneventful period. I can safely say that I am a desert rat in all senses of the word. We in the 7th Arm'd Division have been in*

contact with the enemy all the way from Alamein to Tunis, although I only got back to them at Agheila. When Wavell first pushed in 1940 the 7th Arm'd Division was there and our forward elements were the first in to Tunis. We entered it at 3 o'clock and I myself was there at 3.30, so there are no flies on us. Our journey round from 8th Army was very interesting. We took longer than we meant to, but going through the country that had so much bitter fighting was great fun. When we arrived we were amazed at the beauty and fertility of the land; there was water galore and the 1st Army Canteens were magnificent (I am at the moment smoking Gold Block!). I have told you about my part on May 2nd. We were there for a short time, but there was work to be done and on May 5th we moved *up for the attack. The roads were very dusty and as we moved up it was just like a horse race with the horses moving up to the starting line. The Indians, 8th Army again, were to make the gap, and we were to pass through. Many of the 1st Army were sceptical about our chances of success, but we knew we were going to win. In passing I must say that we should not underestimate the part played by the 1st Army. They held on under appalling conditions when attacked by well organised forces, and if it wasn't for the 1st Army the Allied Forces would have gone right back to Algiers. They hung on like grim death when many of them had never seen action and didn't know the form, and so it isn't surprising that they over-estimated the difficulties of getting through when the opportunity occurred.*

But to return – we passed through at about 9 o'clock, and pushed on like a spear, with a narrow frontage and great power behind. Disregarding pockets of resistance and sidestepping difficulties, we squeezed out the enemy on our flanks, and on the afternoon of the 2nd day I got the first view of Tunis from the hills above it, a great goal reached at last. We went in with the tanks and the whole population turned out to greet us. For three whole days the jubilation went on, but on the next day we had to push North again towards Bizerta; going was easy. We met the Americans in the afternoon and the prisoners flocked in thousands. The loot was quite unparalleled in modern wars. We have captured all they had out here, vehicles, guns, food and everything else. I have got myself a little

"Volkswagen" or "peoples car". It has its engine in the back, is about 10 h.p. and four seater; open but with a folding hood, it is grand as a runabout. I also got a Mercedes Benz staff car, which someone else has now got; it is a beautiful car. But the greatest thing of all is when we heard of a German NAAFI. We at once sent two big 5 ton lorries, and I went to see what we could get. We loaded them both full with food and drink to the value of about £400. Some of their tinned fruits are simply lovely. We also got some black bread, macaroni, sugar, Danish butter, jam and pickles. The only snag is that about 400 civilians (who are a little short of food) came and invaded us. The French gendarmes had their hands full keeping them from pinching the lot. When Tunis has recovered from the Germans it will be

in a very pleasant town. We are now, of course, resting and feeding on the fat of the land. I go up to a farm nearby every day and collect fresh milk and eggs, and they refuse to allow me to pay for it. My French is getting better every day!! Among other things I got from the German NAFFI were 200 bottles of Kummel, which I should think would price at £3 a bottle in England. We are also getting a bit of beer, which I like more than anything else. It's also very pleasant not getting up at crack of dawn. We still get up 0545, but that is considered easy compared with 0345 and 4 o'clock.

No doubt the victory out here has cheered you up, but it is as nothing compared with our satisfaction at having completed a *long campaign and made a name for the 8th Army which will last a long time.*

My love to all,
Andrew

P.S. Have received some of your letters, will answer them soon, many thanks for them, also for the trouble you took over the A.C.

(The AC was an open 2 seater sports car with a dicky which was 1938 vintage and my Father had given it to me for my 21st birthday).

8

Brief Rest in TRIPOLITANIA

"come unto these yellow sands"

Shakespeare.

After a week around Tunis we were ordered back to Tripolitania and retraced our steps along the route we had just come.

We passed through Tripoli where a great Victory Parade had been held for Churchill on 3rd February (not attended by us because we were busy keeping the pressure on the retreating enemy) and established our camp about ten miles east of Homs – the old Roman town of Leptis Magna. We stopped our trucks and put up what tents we had right of the edge of the beach. Since this was now the height of summer it was very hot and the proximity of the sea was a great asset, but you had to leave your shoes at the water's edge because the sand was so hot that you would burn the soles of your feet.

Extract from letter of 25/5/43 – E of Tripoli.

"Well here we are again sitting under the sweltering sun 150 yard's from the deep blue Mediterranean somewhere between Casablanca and Alexandria, so you know exactly where I am!

We actually parked right on the beach and I will be bathing three times a day while we are here. The water is beautifully warm somewhere about 67 degrees. I think and the sand is sparkling white. It is a pity that we are back in the real sweltering heat of an African summer – but why worry when you have the sea on your doorstep? We had an appalling journey; they just wouldn't let us go down the main road but kept sending us down dusty bumpy desert tracks.

Well news is very good thease days; the German towns must be getting very frightened of the R.A.F.

148

raids. You cannot go on dropping big bombs on German towns 24 hours of the day, 7 days a week without something happening. I rather liked Churchill's remark that it hasn't been proved whether air attack only could defeat a country but the experiment was well worth trying! I also thought his idea of Wavell coming over hardly to improve the wealth and happiness of the Mikado of Japan was amusing. We realize that he was speaking in America to Americans but as far as we are concerned we are wishing that he hadn't laid it on quite so thick about their efforts out here, though of course a new army needs success and praise before it gets confidence."

The emphasis was on training and keeping up our efficiency. There was no shortage of training areas in the open desert to the south of us. I perfected a new technique of surveying the gun positions by using the sun as a reference object. It was new, worked well and was very useful later on in Italy - but was not much use in latitudes where the sun was usually hidden by clouds. It was subsequently written up in an Army manual.

The system depended on wireless communication. I would go to some point where I could establish accurately my bearing and would set up my director (theodolite) and make contact by wireless to the three CPOs (Command Post Officers) at the three Batteries and tell them to prepare to shoot the sun. We would then put filters on the eyepieces and I would align my director and then count down over the radio 5, 4, 3, 2, 1, now and then say, after reading my instrument, that was so many degrees, so many minutes. The convention was that we always aimed at the right edge of the sun. It was very accurate and very quick.

For relaxation the Regiment took the lease of a house in Tripoli so that three of four Officers at a time could spend a day or two in the town. Similar arrangements were made for the other ranks. We also had the old Roman amphitheatre at Leptis Magna –remarkably well preserved - and part of the old Roman town much of which is still standing with the great Forum, Temples to various gods and old streets and houses. All this with the backdrop of the blue sea behind. We had one or two Army Entertainment (ENSA) concerts in the amphitheatre with several hundred soldiers occupying the rows of stone seats. On one memorable evening we had Leslie Henson with his 'Green eye of the little yellow god' sketch and also Bee Lillie with her 'Wind round my heart'.

Excerpt from letter 3/7/43 E-Tripoli.

I thought I knew what it was to be hot last year but I didn't! We are now being plagued with a "Khamsin" wind which is southerly wind blowing off the desert. I have never known a wind quite like it.

It is so hot it is like opening an oven door it hits you in the face and you feel as though you are being roasted. My truck is 100yards from the sea and if I come out, I walk back to my truck and my hair is completely dry.

Life is quite intolerable and the sand it blows up and gets everywhere. I think I would slowly pass out if it wasn't for the sea. The temperature yesterday was 115 in the shade and there isn't an awful lot of shade when you are living in the open".

All sorts of sideshows and activities were arranged to keep the troops happy – some more successful than others – but the time passed fairly quickly. I started to think about what I was going to do after the war and decided to switch from Law – which was my first choice – to Engineering, which my father had read at Pembroke, Cambridge 1902 – 1905. I am not sure, looking back, why I decided to make the change but it was possibly because I saw Engineering to be more active and creative and Law more deskbound and less creative. We were being so active at the time that I wanted something equally so.

As an illustration of how simple things were in those days, I got the name of the Admissions Tutor of Pembroke College, Cambridge from my father and wrote to him saying that I wanted to read Engineering and would be ready to come to Pembroke in October 1946 (it was then June 1943) and would he reserve a place for me for that term. He replied that he would if I passed the qualifying exam and in October 1946 I duly turned up and passed the exam. No UCCA in those days!

In retrospect it seems remarkable that I could look forward to the end of the war with so much confidence from as early as June 1943. We knew at that time that an invasion of N. W. Europe would have to be undertaken and the war taken into the German homeland before Hitler would surrender. It was clear that this could not happen before the summer of 1944 and I just allowed a year for this to be effective and another year to get out of the Army. And that is how it happened.

My letter of 6 June gives an idea of the sort of things we got up to. (The hat referred to in the letter eventually reached me nearly a year later).

153

6/6/43

Dear Mother and Father,

Have just received an airletter card dated 23/5; in a footnote to that Father acknowledged receipt of a letter of mine written after the fall of Tunis, for which I am truly grateful. We are all getting a little, not much mind you, but a little bitter about all this talk about the 1st Army capturing Tunis. They didn't, but yet we had no representatives from 8th Army in the Tunis victory parade. But enough of this, it is all very petty. My last letter to you was a long airmail letter in which I disregarded the censor nearly completely as is only reasonable now! On the 28th we had a unique party here. The

154

Colonel, who was in the Sudan Defence Force at one time, got hold of a detachment of Sudanese to give us all an exhibition. They dressed up in horn and necklace and coloured straw pants, with empty tins tied round their legs and sheepskin round their necks (we gave them the sheep in the morning and they killed them at once, ate them and had their skin round their necks in the evening. They did the same to one of our pet rabbits; it made a very good scarf. They started their show with a wrestling bout and then went on to give their war dance. Meanwhile we had invited 50 officers from the division and gave them dinner with whisky and rum punch. It all went down very well and is still talked of. It only cost us £7 - £10 and we had done our entertaining of the division! A few days later we went into our nearby town, saw a football match, a film (in a cinema!), had a bathe off a springboard and pier, had tea and went to a unit variety show and then drove back with headlights full on; altogether most enjoyable. My leave in Tripoli is yet to come and when it does you can be sure that I will tell you all about it. At the moment we are resting on our laurels a bit and on the laurels earned by units who were in the division before we came out here. At the moment everybody is saying nice things anyhow! We have just completed building a kitchen range and oven. We got some fire bricks and earth, added water to the earth to make mud, (no, we didn't have to fetch our own straw, because my name isn't Moses and we didn't use any!!) and then built it up,

156

included an oven and chimney and there we were. We then attached two pipes to two tins, filled one with water and the other with oil and set them dripping into the pan; so now we have a first rate oven. To get to more homely things (I apologise for having to ask for so many things but all you can buy here, if ever you can buy at all, is Italian and worthless), will Father please buy me a round service hat, Khaki, RHA type with brass side-buttons, size 7¼ from Herbert Johnson, 38 New Bond St. They did cost 50/- Explain that I have no coupons and if necessary show them this letter. I will then be most grateful. They will of course do all the posting.

I have just had a letter from Richard; I must write to him personally. How is the brainwork getting on? Slow but sure I should think.

I hear Montgomery was given a great welcome on his last visit to England. He is a very great man but appallingly conceited (and why not?!).

My love to all,

Andrew

However, before long we once again had to think seriously about fighting the enemy. We were not included in the Sicily Campaign but were to be part of General Mark Clark's 5th US Army and invade Italy at a point further up the west coast. This turned out to be Salerno. We duly loaded on to Landing Ship Tanks (LSTs) in Tripoli early in September for our journey to Salerno.

As an illustration of Colonel Peter Gregson's lightness of touch I must recount the events of the last hour or so before we set sail. When all the vehicles were on board

158

he said to me that there was a drinks party that evening at the house of the Brigadier commanding Tripoli district and he and I were going to go. So in our battle clothes and boots we took a jeep – with me driving – and joined this cocktail party with the Brigadier. At about 8 pm Peter Gregson said to me that it was time to go off and invade Italy, so we drove back to the ship where the Port of Authorities were tearing their hair at our absence. After we were on board we set sail – all rather undisciplined, but Peter Gregson was a great man to work for. He retired eventually from the Army as a Major General with two DSO's and one MC and died in the 1990s.

Meanwhile on 8th September news had come through that Italy had thrown in the sponge, but the Germans were going to defend the Italian Peninsular on their own. This did not make as much difference as we thought when we first heard the announcement.

9

Invasion of Italy

"A man who has not been to Italy is always
conscious of an inferiority"
Dr Johnson.

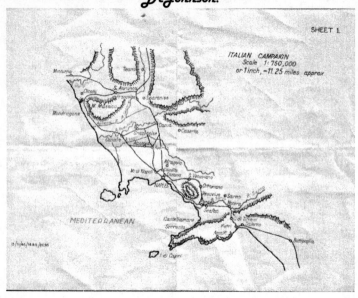

The situation in Italy at this time was that the 8th Army plus US troops, after capturing Sicily, had crossed to the mainland at Messina and were fighting their way north.

Although the Italians had given up, the German forces had been reinforced and were contesting every inch of the way. The Italian peninsular is very much divided by the Apennines into the West and East Coastal plains, so the overall plan was for the 8th Army to push north up the Eastern Coastal plain and the US 5th Army up the Western. Before they divided 8th Army were to relieve the German pressure on Salerno to assist the establishing by 5th Army of a bridgehead. The fact that we were part of US 5th Army didn't make much difference to us since we were also part of the British 10 Corps so that there was a further layer of command between us and Army HQ. And so we embarked on another great adventure.

The Landing Ship was a sizeable vessel, which carried vehicles and tanks on two decks with a steep ramp connecting one to the other. It also had a ramp at the bow for loading and unloading, similar to the modern Roll-on, Roll-off (RORO) vessels.

Our crossing from Tripoli to Salerno took nearly three days and we had air cover to protect us from enemy air attack. When the time came to put us ashore the vessel went full speed ahead for the beach and when about two hundred yards off dropped a kedge anchor from the stern and paid out the cable. We emerged on to the beach more or less dry-shod and the theory was that the ship without its load could pull itself off with its kedge anchor. I have no doubt it was successful but we did not wait to see – we had other things to think about.

The first landing at Salerno was on 9th September and by the time we got there it was about 16th September, partly because the turn around for the ships from Tripoli was seven days so that the build up was, of necessity, slow, and partly because there was not room in the bridgehead for an armoured division until the infantry had done their work. It was, in fact, a bitter battle to establish the bridgehead and the small town of Battipaglia was not taken until just before we arrived.

162

There was quite a lot of enemy air activity at this stage and a lot of noise but very little damage was suffered.

By the 17th September the time had come for us to break out of the bridgehead through the mountainous area to the north and into the Naples Plain. The countryside was very difficult with steeply wooded hillsides and narrow roads with important bridges over rivers. The first attempts at breakout were held up by enemy shellfire and mortar fire on the bridges and defiles and it was not until the 27th that we broke out into the Naples Plain and found ourselves looking up at Mount Vesuvius. We actually had a gun position in Pompeii. We then passed to the NE of Vesuvius while the rest of the Division took the coast road and liberated Naples. Our route took us through Ottavicino and S. Vesuvius towards Afragola.

Before we got through the Vietri Gap there was a lot of waiting on the road, one vehicle behind the other and it was a good thing that by that time we had air cover. What is memorable about those waits is the number of walnut trees alongside the roads. We spent those hours cracking delicious nuts and left the road deep in broken shells when the time came to move on. Also there was a profusion of delightful grapes with a lovely flavour of wild strawberries – Uva fragola.

As we got further north the country became very difficult for operations off the road with vehicles getting stuck in soft ground – a stark change from desert warfare. It was also very difficult for my survey operations because the three Batteries might be in different valleys and it would have been very arduous and time consuming to take a survey traverse from one end to the other. Fortunately the sun was shining on most of the days and I was able to use the system we had practised in the desert and pass the line by radio to each Battery using the sun as a reference object. With heavy rain any movement off the road brought the danger of wheel spins and the four-wheel drive vehicles came into their own. The jeep would go anywhere being very light and having the option of four-wheel drive.

There were a series of rivers which held up our advance, the widest of which was the Volturno, and it took time to establish a foothold of the other side using infantry in boats, then ensuring adequate protection for the Engineers to build a bridge and then bringing the Armour across and pushing on to the next obstacle. It was slow and difficult work.

6 October 1943

Dear Mother and Father,

Just had a few more strawberry grapes so am in a good mood for writing a letter. As far as this campaign has gone I have a very good opinion of it. I am really enjoying myself. The weather and the country are very beautiful and the fruit still continues in its former strength. We usually have a roof over our head at night so if it rains it doesn't really matter. We

165

have had quite an interesting time recently; it hasn't been a walkover but at the same time the resistance hasn't been immensely strong. We have a lot of trouble with ditches and dykes and the country is very dense with fruit trees. There was an interesting little battle the other day. A few infantry – only about 40 – attacked under a barrage laid by us. It all went just as it should have done and was very successful. There was a lot of artillery activity which was made worse by some of our medium guns shelling us too. One landed only about 5 yards from me but I was in an armoured car and quite OK. We had two chickens for dinner next day!

One of our gun positions was in a field recently occupied by the Germans. They had slaughtered all the cows and left the corpses rotting and decomposing close to where we were. The smell was most unpleasant.

On one particular wet evening I had to find some shelter for the HQ party and was exploring along a muddy village lane to find somewhere suitable. Investigating a farm I pushed my way through a large farm door in the middle of a two storey building and found a large open area for the cattle with inches of mud and filth and not much else. Before going I thought I would explore upstairs and found, in contrast, some luxurious accommodation with carpeted floors and nice furniture. So we moved in for a comfortable night. There was only one difficulty; the loos were reached by going back alongside the cattle enclosure, but still on the upper floor. The architect had designed the drainage from the loo to drop straight into the pit where the cattle area drained and so he avoided building a separate system. Unfortunately as sewage decomposes it produces heat and since there was no trap there was a continuous up-draught into our loos so that you had to take some pebbles to weight the paper or else it came up in your face!

By the middle of October we were across the Volturno – in our case by way of a pontoon - Bailey bridge at Capua – and aiming for Mount Massico, an impressive range of hills running nearly up to the sea at its western end. This brought us eventually up to the River Garigliano, which was a major obstacle, and beyond which were the hills leading up to Monte Cassino. However, this was for us the end of our Italian Campaign. Montgomery who had recently been moved back to the UK to command the invasion of France wanted some of his experienced Divisions to come home and lead the invasion forces and we were one of those Divisions. So we stopped short of the River G until replacements arrived to take over from us.

While we were waiting Brigadier Loony Hinde, who was commanding our Brigade, took his Brigade Major with him in a scout car and drove down to the River, despite the fact that it had not so far been cleared of

168

enemy forces. It was a fair assumption that the enemy had withdrawn completely to the other side. However, he was observed by enemy gunners from the other side and they fired a salvo of rounds at him. Since the scout car was a moving target it is not surprising that they missed. But the rounds fell alongside some large ponds by the River and a huge number of duck rose from the water in fright. The Brigadier, who was a keen wildfowler, was astonished to see so many duck. Next day, to the horror of his Brigade Major, he suggested that they would do the same as the day before. He had his sporting gun with him and if the enemy gunners would oblige they would have some good sport. This is exactly what happened; the enemy fired their salvo, the duck flew up and the Brigadier had a good shoot. An unusual form of decoy!

So, for us, the Italian Campaign had been a short one and the ground conditions had not been easy for an Armoured Division; we had had our share of casualties and the wet weather had made life unpleasant. Being taken out of action was not therefore unwelcome and the possibility of going back to England positively attractive. There was of course the added threat of being used as the spearhead of the invasion forces next year but that was some time into the future.

10

RECALLED for D-DAY

"You are ordered abroad as a soldier of the king
To help our French comrades against the invasion
By a common enemy".
Lord Kitchener 1914.

In the second week of December 1943 we moved back
and handed over all our guns and vehicles in the Naples
area and moved to magnificent surroundings in the
Sorrento Peninsular while we waited for transport home.
Our billet was a large house – Casa Greco – on the road
from Castellamare to Amalfi and was high enough to
have glorious views over the Bay of Naples. I think the
plumbing must have been rudimentary because I have a
clear recollection of having a 'slipper' bath of the flat
roof of the house whilst enjoying the view across to the
Isle of Capri. Since it was December I must have been
imagining it – but it was a lovely place.

Extract from letter 26/11/43   Sorrento peninsular Italy.

"It is a very attractive part of the country and the oranges are magnificent. They are one stage better than the Jaffa ones. I am sorry you cannot enjoy them too but they have to be very ripe, then they are bigger than Jaffas, peel like tangerines and they are so juicy that one would fill a tall tumbler. They have been on the tree two years, they must be the acme of their kind in the orange world. Everything is appallingly expensive out here. The people who control the prices need a little instruction in their job. All Christmas cards have gone off I hope they get there in time.

Extract from letter 1/12/43 Sorrento

"So what about the people? I don't know whether it is the climate or the heat but in the Mediterranean countries especially in Italy the people seem to produce children at a most colossal rate. Admittedly fascism

didn't approve birth control, but there is more to it than that.

There are simply thousands of children all badly clothed, mostly underfed but not dangerously underfed, the people themselves are in rather a pathetic state.

They have had to put guns before butter for a long time now and being naturally lazy, untrustworthy and incapable people they resented it. They are still short of food and realize that all their efforts in the past have gained them nothing but the allies treat them as hostile people and their country is being ravaged by the Germans.

I and a couple of others took the opportunity of a two-day trip to Capri, which was a real delight. I had recently been reading the 'Villa of San Michele' by Axel Munthe in which Capri features very prominently and I was also impressed with the old villa of the Emperor Tiberius with its precipitous drop to the sea from the end of the Cypress avenue. On the second evening I slipped and fell on the way <u>out</u> to dinner (not on the way back!) and concussed myself leading to two days in bed on my return to the Caso Greco.

Eventually we embarked at Naples on a small troop ship for our journey home and our only stop was for a few hours at the Algerian port of Oran where the troops did not disembark. Also tied up to the wharf was a huge French battleship – I think it was the 'Lorraine' (or was it 'Richelieu'?) but I am not quite sure – swarming with matelots. Two of us thought we might have a bit of fun,

With all Good Wishes
for Christmas
and the New Year
from

Andrew

Christmas
1943

3rd Regt. R. H. A.
In the Field.

1942	1943
El Mreir	Zuara
Ruweisat Ridge	El Assa
Bare Ridge	Ben Gardane
El Alamein	Medenine
El Aqaqir	Mareth
El Agheila	Wadi Akarit
Wadi Zem Zem	Sfax
Sedada	Djebibina
Tarhuna	Medjez – El – Bab
TRIPOLI	TUNIS

SALERNO

Pompeii	Sparanise
R. Volturno	Mt Massico

R. GARIGLIANO

7th Armoured's Christmas card , 1943

so having got permission to go ashore for half an hour we tried to see how far we could get aboard the French ship before being bundled off again. Carrying our swagger sticks we walked smartly to the gang plank in intense conversation and pretended to return salutes that we had never in fact received and, without a moment's hesitation, walked past the guards at the foot of the gangplank and similarly those at the top and turned left along the quarter deck before a whole party of the

French firmly ushered us ashore again with lots of pretended apologies from us. All good clean fun!

Extract from letter 5/1/44 – Home Forces.

Having spent Christmas day on board we arrived at Greenock early in the New Year and travelled by train to Norfolk where we were to spend our next five months. Within a few days we were allowed on leave and I came home for the first time for nearly two years. The leave was for fourteen days and we made the most of it. Most of my leave was spent at home in Somerset with some winter tennis and riding horses on the Mendip Hills, but the rest of it in London where my father was then working Monday to Friday. According to my diary we saw 'Jane Eyre' and 'For whom the Bell Tolls' and, as a play, 'Arsenic and Old Lace'. London was still a place for entertainment and restaurants though everything was very dark at night with no streetlights and no illuminated signs. You had to know where you were going. As far as I can remember the bombing at that time was not significant; there were a few months to go before the first V1 – Doodlebugs – became a nuisance. A lot of the London Clubs made their rooms available to serving officers and I recall one night at the National Liberal Club where the most memorable feature was the immense bath with a red line painted at the four-inch level so as to dissuade you from taking too much hot water.

Trains were fairly frequent but not normally very punctual and sometimes it was difficult to find out the destination of the train. Once at Didcot I had to go to the Locomotive and ask the driver whether he was going to Cardiff or Bristol. On the roads you needed to have a good map because most of the signposts had been removed.

It was a wonderful relaxation to be home again after so long and I am sure my parents were relieved to see me safe and sound even though it was only temporary. It was only after the war that I began to see how much of a strain it was for parents to have a son fighting a war in foreign parts. This was brought home to me very vividly when, many years later, my father told me that when the village had a party to celebrate the end of the European war on 8 May 1945 my mother would not come because she had not had a letter from me for ten days and so could not be sure that I was still alive. I had been fairly careful to write at least once in ten days but it had sometimes been difficult to do so and, in any case, you were not allowed to say anything in your letters! We had the tiresome job of censoring our men's letters to make sure no security was breached; they all finished with SWALK or ITALY. In December 1943 they started to use BURMA and we had to find out what it stood for. The answer was "be upstairs ready my angel"!

The atmosphere in England in January 1944 was purposeful and impressive. There was complete singleness of purpose in wanting to wage war on our enemies and resist attacks and withstand misfortune.

People helped each other to a remarkable degree and everyone had something positive to do. The country was full of troops – especially Americans and Canadians preparing for "Overlord" – code name for the Normandy invasion - and it was once joked that the country would have sunk into the sea if it had not been kept afloat by the Barrage Balloons!

On my return from leave I found that I was posted to K Battery as Command Post Officer (CPO) and my vehicle was a Sherman Tank. Our towed guns had been replaced with ones mounted on a tank chassis, so a new drill had to be learnt to handle them. The new equipment was called a "Sexton" and it consisted of the normal 25 pdr gun being mounted on a Canadian Ram Tank chassis from which the turret had been removed. It had advantages and disadvantages over our familiar towed guns. The prime advantage was that it could traverse ground that would have been impassable to wheeled vehicles and was very quick to bring into action. Its disadvantages were that it had only 20° either way top traverse on its gun so that to engage a target outside this range the whole "tank" had to move. This took time, caused inaccuracy and turned the ground into a mud bath. But the gun crew had better protection from enemy shell fire. Most of our time was spent in training to become familiar with our new equipment and – in my case and others – our new jobs. My job as CPO was to take charge of the Battery gun position – to ensure that the two troops of four guns each were properly deployed and accurately aligned and positioned according to the map. Of the two Officers senior to me in the Battery, the Battery Commander (a Major) would be forward with the formation we were supporting and the Battery Captain whose responsibilities were administration and supplies etc might be anywhere.

We felt the need to be friendly with the Russians at this stage and our CO Peter Gregson arranged for two or three very senior Russian Officers, who were part of a military mission at Kings Lynn, to be our guests at a formal dinner in the Mess. I was detailed to go and pick them up, which I did, but conversation was nearly zero since we could find no common language. The dinner went off well enough and I am sure they found it every bit as strange as we did in entertaining them. We drank to the heroic Russian Army with heroic quantities of Port and Whisky and, not surprisingly, I cannot remember how we got them home.

Our nearest village was Brandon and the nearest town Thetford and time passed very quickly. It was not long before we started to waterproof our vehicles – most of them up to a depth of four feet and some even more. Each type of vehicle was provided with its own kit for the job and this would include light metal tubes to enable the air intakes to be taken above the planned water level and similarly for the exhausts. Insulating covers would be stuck on to the distributor and over the plugs etc. In the case of wheeled vehicles the driver would probably get his feet wet but for tanks the water had to be kept out of the hull and any place where the water could get in was covered with waterproof material. In the case of my Sherman tank the air intake for the engine was by way of the turret so this needed no protection but the exhaust had to be extended. We had a vehicle 'sheep dip' into which we drove them to check the efficiency of the waterproofing. In the case of tanks there was a technique of removing some of the waterproof covers after landing without getting out of the tank. This was achieved by placing some coils of explosive under the covers and wiring these to a plug, which could be put into its socket by the driver. In most cases – and certainly in mine – when we arrived on shore in Normandy we had enough bangs already, so we chose a good moment to tear off the covers and throw away the explosive. But not so our Brigadier Commander Royal Artillery (CRA) who fired his off in the prescribed way and shattered nearly all the bottles in his case of Whisky which he had acquired at great cost and packed on the back of his tank.

But I am now getting ahead of my story. Sometime in May we left Brandon and moved to Orwell Park near

Ipswich where we were all 'confined to Barracks' until the invasion started. This was a pleasant enough place and we managed to find enough to do to fill the hours. Eventually on one of the early days of June we left Orwell Park all loaded up with ammunition and stores and moved down towards Felixstowe. The movement planning was incredibly thorough and each vehicle was given a number and had to find that number painted on the road and stop there until the column of vehicles moved on. This ensured that not all the vehicles of one unit were on the same ship and it also put us into the right order for embarking on to the Landing Ships. Eventually the column moved forward and we found ourselves on a very similar vessel to the one from which we had landed at Salerno. As soon as we were all aboard the ship left Felixstowe and we went to sea. We could not tell where we were but on 6th June we were obviously making for the French coast and in every direction in which you looked there were vessels of all shapes and sizes steaming south with aircraft overhead to give us cover. The weather was fairly calm and we were full of confidence. Ironically the book I was reading was ' A Thousand Shall Fall' by Habe.

I suppose that the atmosphere was fairly tense on board as we prepared to land on enemy territory and withstand all that they threw at us but we were not inexperienced. We had done this before and each of us knew what our particular job was to be. Meanwhile there was a lot to look at. The Channel was alive with activity and you felt part of something very big and very historic. To land in Normandy at any time in that first week would be memorable, but to be watching the vanguard approaching the coast on day one was very exciting.

So many years after the event it is easier to remember what you did than how you felt. If you were to be approaching this sort of operation on your own then fear and anxiety would be uppermost but we were part of a large and experienced team and were confident. In addition we had trust in our commanders. Over the last two years we had had no serious setbacks and by and large what our commanders had foretold had in fact come to pass. So we now felt fairly sure that this invasion was going to be successful and that all possible precautions had been taken. If Montgomery was in charge, then all would work out as planned.

11

D-Day and Villers Bocage

"A battle there was, which I saw, man"
McLennan.

This was D-day and we expected to go ashore that evening but we hit a sand bar and the decision was made for us to go ashore next day. We were being kept informed about how things were going and we could see that on our sector things were not too noisy. For the most part we just had to trust that this delay in going ashore was part of a sound plan and that we would be able to reach our objectives soon after.

There was no gunfire coming our way and we splashed into about three-foot of water on D-day plus 1 on Gold Beach. Compared with the horrors of Omaha Beach we had an easy landing. The 50th Division (TT – Tyne & Tees) had cleared the area so that we could at once move south to Bayeux and beyond. It is vitally

186

important on these sort of occasions that people know exactly what to do and where to go. The answer to the first is clear orders in advance and, for the second, to have routes clearly marked and the Divisional Military Police take this on as their responsibility. Each formation had its sign and in our Division the red Desert Rat – and below that Brigade and Regiment have a number. Our Regiment number was 76 with the two colours blue and red, and to differentiate still further a red quadrant would be in different corners of the square to indicate which Battery. So, as we came ashore, we followed the signs appropriate to ourselves and our guns came into action somewhere near Bayeux.

The first few days on our part of the front were devoted to building up our resources with more and more ships arriving off the beaches and discharging further troops, ammunition and other supplies. One of my memories is hearing the huge sixteen-inch shells from *HMS Rodney* passing overhead. She was lying a short distance off shore and the noise of these shells passing over was like a passenger train; I don't know where they were landing or what damage they were doing.

The countryside we now found ourselves in was very different from the rolling open plains one normally associates with Northern France. In contrast this Bocage country was well wooded with hedges and orchards and very limited visibility. It was ideal for defence but very difficult for attack. The military planners had hoped that we would be through this belt of terrain before we had to engage seriously with the enemy.

On the morning of the 10th we started on our planned attack south to Villers Bocage and beyond. Progress over the first three days was slow but continuous with the enemy having to be cleared out of one strong point after another, but eventually, early in the morning of the 13th, the tanks of the 4th County of London Yeomanry (CLY) entered Villers Bocage and their leading squadron went through to the high ground beyond. At this moment they came up against a German Armoured Division coming north to attack the bridgehead. So

188

started the Battle of Villers Bocage which has been the subject of various books and which I am not in a position to describe in any detail. I can only tell what I saw of it.

The leading squadron of 4th CLY was surrounded and overwhelmed by the German armour and was forced to surrender and be taken prisoner. With them was Billy Dunlop, one of our Troop Commanders and Forward Observation Officer (FOO). He also was captured. The HQ of the 4th CLY and another squadron was trapped on the narrow street of the village and their tanks were knocked out one by one by a German Tiger tank which was impervious to the guns of our Cromwells. The German Tank Commander was Michael Wittman and this action demonstrated not only his courage but also the effectiveness of the Tiger tank. The CLY tanks could not turn in the narrow street, nor could they reverse because of the tanks behind them – and in any case the Cromwell's maximum speed in reverse is only about 2 mph – nor could they damage the German tank by firing at it because their 75mm armour piercing shells just bounced off. One or two managed to turn off into side streets but none were able to knock out Wittman's tank. Most of the crews managed to bail out before their tanks were hit. Subsequently another squadron of 4 CLY and a company of the Queens Regiment came in to stop the rot and something like 12 Tiger tanks were knocked out. Wittman survived this action but was killed later on in the campaign. Our Battery Commander had to abandon his tank, which was destroyed, and so did our other Troop Commander – Paddy Victory. This effectively stopped our advance and during the rest of this day and the next our armour and infantry did battle with the enemy and though we eventually had to abandon Villers Bocage the enemy lost more tanks than we did.

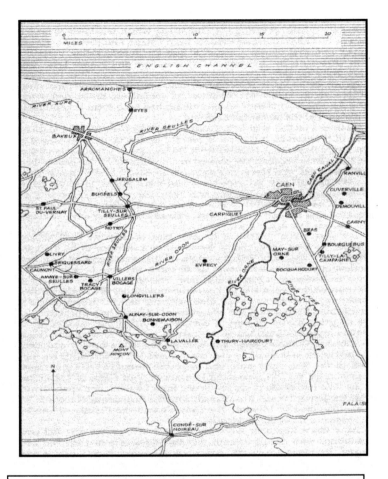

7th Armoured Division in Normandy

Meanwhile we came into action just short of the village and engaged targets as they presented themselves. We imagined that the enemy might launch an attack on us down the road from the village and were prepared to engage the tanks over open sights but the attack did not materialize. That night our Brigade formed a box for our defence – so as to resist attacks from all directions - but it passed off quietly.

I remember that on that evening we were told that we were going to maintain our position and I was given the opportunity to move back further into the box because at present we were on the front edge of it. But the guns were sited in a strong position with the crest of the hill about 100yards in front so that we could engage enemy tanks as they came over the crest and before they saw us. So I said we would stay where we were. I took my sleeping bag up to No. 1 gun position for the night to give them confidence. In the event the enemy did not attack.

Where we were the terrain was gently rolling with quite a lot of trees and hedges. The road from Villers Bocage towards us dropped down into a small valley and then rose again to a point just in front of us. Our guns were on this reverse slope with a small stream behind us and then some trees. Because we were so short of Firefly tanks (with 17 pdr guns) our 25 pdrs with AP (Armour Piercing) shot were probably the most effective way of knocking out a Tiger, so our position was a good one.

The Brigadier, Loony Hinde, called a conference that evening when things were fairly tense. When everyone was assembled and they were ready to start Loony interrupted everything by asking for an empty matchbox. Everyone was mystified but a matchbox was provided. Loony started crawling on the ground to capture a moth. Mike Carver who was there (later Field Marshal Lord Carver) said "Loony, we have got vital things to discuss and great urgency. This is no time to be chasing moths". But Loony replied "Mike, you can have a tank battle any day of the week, but you will see this type of moth only once in a lifetime"!

The decision was made next day for us to withdraw several miles as long as we were not being attacked and that this should take place by night. This was duly done and all our vehicles followed each other through the darkness until we reached the relative safety of another Division's forward defended location.

It has been argued that instead of withdrawing us the Army should have reinforced us and used Villers Bocage as a jumping off place for a very much earlier capture of Caen, but there must have been strong arguments against this. The destruction of 12 or more of our tanks in the village illustrates how under-gunned we were. The only gun that would knock out a Tiger was our 17 pdr but we had only a few of these. In each troop of four tanks one was a Sherman Firefly which had a 17 pdr, but the others had 75mm guns with much less

'My Most Dreadful Ten Hours'

Cpl. Leonard Payne, of Bristol, who took part in the Normandy fighting near Villars-Bocage, told a reporter, "Never in the desert or in Italy did we have such close fighting."

He tells the story of 10 hours that started with disaster and ended with the smashing of the great German panzer threat to the Allied positions near the village.

They were "the most dreadful ten hours" ever spent by his unit.

It began by the Germans carving up the regimental headquarters.

Nazi Tank

The unit was rushed forward when a German Panther tank crept through a wood on the left.

"The German tank let 10 of our tanks go by and then knocked out a troop carrier full of our soldiers," said Cpl. Payne.

"Then he came up the road, knocking out some headquarters and tanks and got our communication staff, the medical people and nearly everything connected with headquarters.

Knocked Out

"When he had finished mowing down our men with machine-gun fire he turned round and drove off with the commander standing in the turret waving his hand and bowing."

But that is only the first part of the story for the Seventh Armoured Division came back and repulsed a massive attack from the S.S. Panzer Division—the pick of Hitler's youth.

Six Tigers were knocked out one after another.

"But the thing I shall remember longest," Cpl. Payne said, "was the sight of our leader, Lt. Cotton, peeping round the corner of a Tiger from beneath an umbrella and taking snapshots."

"Desert Rats" in Normandy

Still Chasing Rommel

It was fully expected that the famous "Desert Rats" would come into the limelight again, and the announcement that they are serving in France will give pride and pleasure to us at home, and particularly to those who followed their remarkable story in the North African campaigns.

Their encounters with the enemy also included some of severest fighting on the Salerno beaches.

No doubt, writes the "Evening World" London Correspondent, some of the experience they gained in that battle was a valuable asset in the Normandy landings.

To the story of their tenacity and determination — demonstrated to the full at El Alamein and in Tunisia—is now to be added a chapter which is likely to be equally remarkable. Ranged before against Rommel's Afrika Korps, they now stand face to face with Rommel's men on the Continent.

Men who are now in France tasting their first battlefield struggle with the enemy will profit by the experience of the "Desert Rats."

At home, the fact that the Seventh Armoured Division—to give the "Rats" their more formal designation—are fighting in Normandy will inspire confidence.

A.T.A. Officer Dies

The death is reported on active service of Henry John Norman Rowe, first officer, Air Transport Auxiliary, of 15, Nithsdale-rd., Weston-s-Mare.

195

hitting power. There were no Fireflies to resist the Tiger in the main street of the village, though one scared Wittman off.

The Battle had been neither a victory nor a defeat but it was certainly a missed opportunity. One thing it did achieve was to blunt the attack of the German armour,

which might otherwise have caused major problems on the perimeter of the bridgehead.

Extract from letter 29/6/44   Normandy.

"You were right in guessing that we were out here early on. We arrived off the beaches late on D Day and disembarked on D+1 Things were very quiet on the whole and it was nothing like as fierce as we thought it was going to be. I cannot tell you much about what we have done except refer to the Villas Bocage incident because that was reported fully. We had quite a tense couple of days I reckoned that we did the enemy a lot of damage and strategically disturbed him a lot, but moiré

about that in due course of time. Our main trouble at the moment is sleep a lack of it"

A certain amount of reorganization was needed on our return from Villers Bocage. We had lost our Battery Commander – he received only minor wounds but had to be evacuated - and one of the Troop Commanders was a POW. I was promoted to Captain as one of the Troop Commanders and two new men came into the Battery to fill the other posts.

My new job – and the one I did for the rest of the campaign – was to command the troop of four guns, about seventy-five men altogether. This was, in theory, my responsibility but the actual job was not to be with the guns but to be with whatever formation of tanks or infantry we happened to be supporting at that time. The main tank Regt was 4CLY who were shortly after replaced by 5th Inniskilling Dragoon Guards (5DG). The infantry in our case were 1st Rifle Brigade and the Armoured Car Regiment the 11th Hussars. We also had the 8th Hussars as an additional Armoured Regiment. I received my orders from the Battery Commander as to which Regiment I was to support and where I would find them.

My transport was now a Cromwell tank, which was the same tank as used by the Armoured Regiment so that when travelling with them I could not be distinguished as the Artillery Officer. I had a driver and co-driver, who was also the cook, and machine gunner and two signallers with me in the turret. Although we had the same 75mm gun in the turret as the other tanks, it was not intended to be used by us in an offensive role and the signallers were not trained as gunners; each signaller was responsible for one number nineteen set; the first was tuned into my Battery frequency for communication with the guns and the second tuned in to the formation I was supporting. So spread out on the turret in front of me were three headsets – the third being for communication with the driver – and I had to be careful to use the right one on each occasion.

Generally speaking my tank crew remained the same, although changes had to be made from time to time. We were together all the time, we fed together and we slept together and we were all involved in the same jobs of providing artillery support for the tanks or infantry as the case may be. As a result we got to know each other very well and relationships were very relaxed. Clearly I was the leader but it was never necessary to 'pull rank'. I remember one very cold day when I had a new signaller in the tank. At one stage when I was very busy speaking on my headset I noticed him taking off his tank suit – a very effective kapok lined suit issued to tank crews. This zipped up from foot to collar and was put on like a coat. I asked him what he was doing and he said he wanted a pee. Since there was a short zip in the appropriate place I told him there was a gadget for this purpose – not a very meaningful comment – and five minutes later I found him peering around the turret looking for an en-suite loo!

One of the problems of being a tank commander was travelling on tracks and roads already congested with infantry on foot. No soldier slogging along the road wants to be ordered to make way for a tank and my solution to this was to fix a bell, which I had found somewhere, onto my tank turret and this made exactly the noise of a Glasgow tram. So whenever I rang it the troops were amused at the sound of it rather than angry at being pushed aside. I called my tank Ariadne but I can't think why!

The normal pattern was for me to locate the formation to which I was assigned and find out from them where our guns could be of any value. There were a number of alternatives and in some cases the CO would want me to stay near him so that I could bring fire to bear where it was required. This would be done entirely on a map reference basis, or I would be directed to one of their squadrons or companies and perform the same function there. More frequently I would be told where the main pressure was and asked to get myself into a position where I could observe the enemy and if possible break up their formations before they could launch an attack or deal with a pocket of resistance.

If the choice was to find an observation point (OP) then one had to look around for some place from where one would have an observation without being too obvious. If it involved climbing a tree or going into an upper floor of a building or a hedge on the crest of a hill, then I would leave my tank at the nearest safe place and out of sight, take a control box with trailing telephone wires up to my vantage point and give my orders to the guns direct.

The business of directing fire on to your chosen target is an art, which has to be learnt. The guns are hardly ever directly behind you and account had to be taken of the effect of a change in line or a change in range. Because you are very seldom looking down on the ground in front it is important to get a round to land on a line between you and the target so that the smoke from the bursting shell can clearly be seen as this side of the target or beyond. Once you have achieved this you alter the line and range together (you have to do your sums) until you have bracketed the target on what is called the line OT (observer > target).

At nightfall you had to agree with your infantry/armour as to where they wanted their Defensive Fire targets (DF) for the night. These would be given a name so that if there was an emergency during the night they only had to call for that name and the fire would come down without delay in the prescribed area. Recording these DF tasks was quite laborious because first you had to agree with your hosts where they should be and what they should be called and then you had to get on to your radio and get this information down to the guns. Unfortunately radio communication was always worst at sunset because, apparently, the Heavyside layer descends at this time of day and one gets a lot of interference.

This done you would probably have something to eat and spend the night with the commander of your armour/infantry. I remember with the 11th Hussars I always discussed with the Squadron Leader as to whether it was a pyjama night or not according to the likelihood of a peaceful or disturbed night. We nearly always got it wrong!

The days were fairly long. You had to be up and about before first light and there were not many opportunities for relaxation during the day if you were manning an observation point. It was frequently after dark before you had finished recording the Defensive Fire tasks and had something to eat. So you would get to bed by about 10.30 and be up at 4.30 am. After a few days of this you were in urgent need of rest and as soon as a replacement for you came up you could go back to the gun area and sleep the clock round.

As gunners we had one difficult problem with DF tasks. If the guns were fairly far back (our maximum range was twelve thousand yards) – or if the fire was called for in the middle of their zone, there was no particular problem and the fire came down fairly quickly and accurately. The guns got a meteorological message every four hours, which enabled them to correct for temperature or wind change. But if the guns were fairly close up or the target was at the edge of their zone, then they could not reach the target using the top traverse of their gun and it was necessary to start up the tank and by forward and reverse get it back on its platform but differently aligned. This was all right in theory, but in practice they would never get it back on exactly the same platform and since at night the guns worked on a reference object, which was a hurricane lamp in a tin with a slot in it on a nearby tree rather than the distant object they used by day, there would be a sizeable error of alignment. This meant that the shells came down late and in the wrong place. Your hosts would be quite rude to you – especially if they were coming down on their heads.

Despite these difficulties you did your best to give help in the place it was required and at the right time. Generally speaking we got things right and it could often be very helpful. In the process you got to know the people very well and they got better at realizing what you could do and what you couldn't. When on the move you often travelled with the leading squadron, but it was one of them rather than you who was 'first around the corner'. These were the men who really showed courage. When you never know whether an enemy tank or an 88 is waiting for the first of your tanks to come round the corner, it takes real courage to be that tank.

Although it may sound presumptuous it is probably not an exaggeration to say that my presence gave considerable strength to any small body of troops.

Because you were there you could bring down fire exactly where it was needed, very quickly. If for instance you had recorded a likely target by ranging on to it with gunfire earlier in the day, you could bring down shellfire on this target again within 1 vor 2 minutes.

It would be impossible – and tedious if possible – to give a blow by blow account of this period of June and July. We moved from one sector to another and were not major players in Operation Goodwood, which was a thrust by Armoured Divisions at the eastern end of the bridgehead. Our role was to pass through the hole punched by the other Divisions, but since they did not succeed in punching a hole, we had no role to play and returned to the Aunay-sur-Odon sector.

In my letter home of 21 July 1944, I referred to one of the problems.

> *... It is still wet here but it isn't the wet that is causing most irritation at the moment, but the mosquitoes. They are as bad as they were in Italy and now we haven't got the same antidotes and preventions as we had then. Some people can't sleep at all because of them and others who can, as can I, wake up with literally hundreds of bites all over our*

face. It is really most unpleasant. We had
a colossal shower of rain yesterday which
is being continued intermittently now and
the ground is one large sea of mud. I am
very glad of my gumboots. I must say that
I am very sorry for the infantry; in this
weather they must lead an absolute dog's
life.

It was about this time that I lost my tank, but in many ways was very lucky. The 4th CLY had recently been replaced by the 5DG and I was in my tank behind a hedge, engaging targets as they presented themselves, when we were shelled by some enemy field guns. These are not likely to do you much damage if you are in a tank unless you get a direct hit, so I kept my head down until it stopped. The tanks who were not far away from me misinterpreted the danger from the shellfire – having only recently arrived from the UK – and thought it was from anti-tank guns. Accordingly they started their engines and moved back a short distance without my

207

noticing it. I suddenly realized that I was on my own and rather vulnerable. So I came back through this large field, through a hedge and into a lane. At this point there was a track going into the wood that bordered the lane so I told my driver to reverse into this track for a short distance where we could stop and see what was happening. Very soon after there was a great bang and machine gun fire at us from behind. This was closely followed by clouds of smoke and, thinking that the tank was on fire, I ordered my crew to bale out and get into the ditch on the other side of the lane. We did this and soon after the smoke died down. We then realised that the tank was not on fire but that a Panzerfaust infantry anti-tank weapon had hit the tank and set off our smoke generators. The tank engine was still running. So I told the driver to get back into the driver's seat using the turret to shield him from fire and from view since we were probably being observed from the wood in the rear and to drive the tank on to the road where we would come aboard. This he did and we made our way back without interference. After a short distance my driver told me that his feet were in water; so clearly the rocket had damaged the cooling system, but we got back to safety before the engine seized up. A new tank came later in the day.

We were still in this area a few days later on 3rd August when we were at the receiving end of some more enemy shelling. Unfortunately we were in an orchard and one of the shells hit a tree and burst several feet above ground level. These airbursts are always more dangerous since the fragments cover a wider area than one bursting in the ground and one of those fragments hit me in the right shoulder. It was not a major injury in any way and I imagined that after a dressing I could continue as before. However, I was persuaded to go back to the MO who was not too far away and this I did. Rather to my surprise he sent me to the Field Hospital for an x-ray and this was the beginning of another story.

At this point I wrote to my parents.

Extract from letter 5th May Normand

"I have been wounded again- silly I know but there it is. This time in the right shoulder slight and I don't think the bone has been damaged at all. The fact that I can write at all is proof of that. It was a shell again and a very u8nlucky one. It was all by itself, no others landed before it and none after. We were standing around my tank when it arrived and a small piece the size of a pea went into my shoulder from the front.It might have been a lot worse. I am writing this from a general hospital in France and I think it is odds on that I will be evacuated to England. I am due to have an x ray this afternoon just to see whethee the bone has been damaged or no and where the piece of metal is. I am feeling perfectly well myself and eating heartily so you need have no fear this time "

But before I continue with that story, I must refer to something that happened in the Division at about the time I was being evacuated - this is the night of the long knives. This account is based on what I was told when I rejoined my Regiment four months later. It appears that the Division was ordered to attack Aunay-sur-Odon "at all costs" and that such an attack against a very strong enemy position would have resulted in very heavy casualties without any certainty of success. What happened then I do not know but the attack did not take place in that form and as a result there was a complete clear out of all officers in the Division, Lieutenant-Colonel and above. The Divisional Commander Bobby Erskine went and was replaced by Major General Verney. 'Loony' Hinde went, the CRA, Ray Mews and our CO Peter Gregson, who was replaced by Paddy Moore.

Clearly the Army Commander General Dempsey had decided that a shake-up was required in the Division and that was his preferred way of doing it. To what extent it was justified is another question. There was no case of the Division of having lost its nerve but it is probably true that having been in action for so long it was being more "canny" than some formations for whom Normandy was their first action. Maybe the sort of order they received at Aunay-sur-Odan took too little account of the position on the ground in their view.

Whatever it was we lost some commanders for whom we had great respect and although I wasn't there at the time I am sure it had an effect on morale.

12

Walking Wounded – August 1944

O God of Battles! Steel my soldier's hearts
Shakespeare.

The Field Hospital was a collection of tents and I was taken there feeling rather bogus, but accepting that if a piece of metal goes in and doesn't come out again it is reasonable to have a look at where it has got to.

I was there for twenty-four hours and having seen the x-ray they decided to evacuate me to the UK. I found this even more amazing but these Field Hospitals have to move their patients on as fast as possible in case there is a sudden rush of casualties.

The story of what happened then is told in Chapter 1, the shipwreck and the loss of trousers!

After a relatively short time I was up and about with a smart new pair of trousers and on the 17th August went into Glasgow and among other things had a meal with the parents of Billy Dunlop who had been taken prisoner at Villers Bocage. By this time they had heard that he was safe and in a POW camp but they were glad to have had contact through me. There was however, one misfortune on that day in that I missed seeing someone who had come a long way to see me. In Chapter 2 I referred to joining the Glosters with David Sinclair. His father was appointed Director General of Army Requirements in 1940 and subsequently the Representative of the Minister of Supply in Washington and it was while they were there that I wrote to them from Tunisia to sympathize with them when I heard that David had been killed at Alamein. By August 1944 they were back in London and hearing that I was in hospital at Killearn, Lady Sinclair had come all that way to see me. The matron had omitted to tell her that I was that day, with full permission, spending the day in Glasgow. It was unfortunate.

David had been of the same age as me and though we had been to different schools we had learnt to read and write together at his house before school and being neighbours had seen a lot of each other in the holidays. We had the two months together with the Glosters and when I left to go to OCTU and then join the RHA, he also went to OCTU and then joined the Black Watch. At that time a new regiment was being formed called the Reconnaissance Regiment and David transferred to that. It was while he was with that Regiment that he was killed at Alamein.

By 18 August I was discharged from hospital. I was allowed a week's leave at home, which I enjoyed very much and then had to make my way to the RA Depot at Woolwich where I started on the long and arduous task of getting back to my Regiment.

At that time the Depot was very much a transit camp with people coming and going all the time. They tried to keep us busy by involving us in the sort of training activities that I described in my diary at the time as 'Military Amusements'. It was all very unreal. But less unreal was the bombing. On the first Sunday I got up early to go to the 8am Communion at the Depot Church having noticed the time of service from the notice board outside the Church. When I got there just before 8am I pushed the door open and there was no church. The façade was undamaged but the rest had been destroyed by bombs some weeks earlier.

This was also the time of the V1 Doodlebugs and they were coming over quite frequently. You could hear the familiar sound of their engines and as soon as you heard them cut out you tended to get yourself close to a bolthole in case it came down in your vicinity.

I wanted to get things moving about my future and getting little change out of the C.O. at Woolwich, I telephoned and arranged a meeting with a Brigadier RA at the War Office. Brigadier Duncan was a delightful man and we talked about the Normandy Campaign and he said that he would do what he could but meanwhile he would post me to 6th RHA in Essex who were, in effect, a holding Regiment through whom reinforcements were sent on to the active RHA

Regiments. So after some more leave I made my way to Wickham Market and joined 6th RHA on 27 September.

I decided to try one more visit to the War Office and once again saw the Brigadier Duncan who tried to persuade me to stay with the 6 RHA. I told him that without being immodest I thought my Regiment would rather see me, who was experienced and knew all their ways, than having to train up a new man who had no experience. As a last shot he offered me what could have been seen as a plum job – ADC to General 'Jumbo' Maitland-Wilson in Cairo. My father never understood why I turned this down but, at the time the war was far from being won and I thought my place was with my Regiment rather than a staff job in Cairo, where I would be organizing Cocktail parties for the General (later Field Marshal) – or so I thought! So in the end he relented and I got my posting back to 5RHA, leaving London on 21 October.

I suppose that Duncan's concerns were twofold. Partly he thought that I had already done enough and partly he had a number of well qualified captains who had not yet seen any action, impatient to be given a posting to a Regiment like 5 RHA.

13

Belgium and pursuit of the enemy

"It may be in you smoke concealed

Your comrades chase e'en now the flyers

And but for you possess the field"

Clough

We embarked at Southampton for an overnight journey to Ostend where, after spending a night at the Transit Camp, we caught a train the next day to Louvain where we stayed for three nights. We were billeted in private houses and on the second evening I asked if we could have a bath. I was told this was not possible but was given the address of an adjacent house which had a bathroom available. At this time I was with Robert Armitage who was also a Captain in K Battery and like me was returning to the Regiment. The two of us knocked on the door and the lady of the house showed us up to the bathroom – a fairly small room with bath, basin and a gas geyser for heating the water. We tossed for first bath and Robert won; so while he bathed I washed my socks in the basin. After a few minutes he complained of feeling wuzzy and thought the water must have been too hot. Soon after saying this he collapsed in a heap on the floor and I realized that I was not feeling too well myself. Fortunately I had the presence of mind to realize that we were being gassed and pushing Robert away from the doorway managed to open the door and get some fresh air before having to sit down myself. With the benefit of a draught of clean air Robert revived and we realized that we had been very lucky. The houseowners were, of course, very concerned and they were probably lucky also because if this had happened a month or two earlier with two German Officers they might not have got away with it so easily. We told them that we regarded it as an accident.

From Louvain we moved on to Bourg Leopold for one night and from there rejoined the Regiment. Much to my delight I was immediately given my old job back as Troop Commander of E/F Troop and Robert was my opposite number with the other Troop. Once again I was succeeding Paddy Victory who went to RHQ as Adjutant of the Regiment having recently been awarded an immediate M.C.

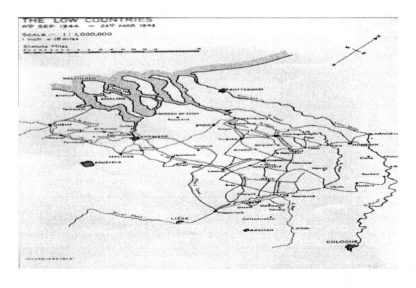

The Low Countries

On the day after my arrival I was on the job and with the 5DG who were trying to push the enemy back in the area of Vaart. This was all part of an operation to clear the enemy from the area between Tilburg and S'Hertogenbosch. It was all very flat open ground with lots of canals and drainage ditches and only a mile or two from the River Maas which was our next major obstacle and which the enemy were defending in the hope that once winter set in we would not be able to operate effectively and they would have time to reorganize. It was difficult to find cover from view and I lost one of my tank crew from shellfire on this operation.

I remember the incident clearly. I and my crew were outside our tank and talking with one of the infantry commanders when we were obviously seen by an enemy gunner who brought his guns to bear on us and some shell fire came down without warning. The only casualty was my signaller - name Philips – and though he was hit it didn't seem too serious. He was evacuated with the minimum of delay but his wounds were more serious than we thought and he died the next day.

On the 10th November the whole Division was moved south and travelling by way of Turnhout we arrived at Weert after a very unpleasant night journey. For the rest of November, all December and part of January the Division's role was to hold the line on the right hand flank of the 2nd Army's sector, first on the west and subsequently on the east bank of the Maas. This involved a limited amount of movement since the going was so difficult, but for me I was moving from one formation to another and finding places from which I could observe and engage targets – mainly infantry in the open or moving vehicles.

At the beginning of December the Battery moved to the small village of Born north of Maastricht and I had an OP at a small farmstead called Gebroek which I occupied on and off for five weeks or so while there was no major activity on our part of the front. This was basically one large barn and one or two smaller buildings alongside. One could only approach it during the hours of darkness because the approach road was open to view from the other side. Some of the tiles had been blown off the roof and my 'perch' was in the loft in a position from where I could see through the opening without being too close so that others could see me. It was fairly tedious most of the time though I did do one or two interesting shoots into 'dead' ground with cross observation from another battery OP; one of these involved ranging with airburst so that one could see the shells bursting rather than lose them in dead ground..

The guns and the rest of the Battery were in the village of Born – about three miles back – and the officer's mess was comfortably established in a large family house close to a level crossing. The family name was Obdenkampf and the father used to manage a brickworks but had had an industrial accident and was disabled. His wife ran the house with their four daughters aged between eight and thirteen. They were living in the basement for safety and so were quite happy to let us use the other floors. They all spoke excellent English and it was a good arrangement for everyone. They were very short of food at the time so some of our supplies found their way to the basement on a fairly regular basis. For us who were existing in an entirely male environment it was pleasant to be involved with a family for a few weeks. In 1996 my wife and I were in Holland and we found the house in Born and made contact with one of the two surviving daughters now living near Amsterdam. She told me that for them those few weeks were very special and as we drove off in January they watched from the window and one of the girls said to her mother "Couldn't we have another little war so that these nice English Officers could stay with us again?" These are some nice memories even from a predominantly horrid time.

One evening I was having a slipper bath on the top floor when I heard the explosions from a stick of bombs each one getting nearer and nearer to where I was. I decided that there was absolutely nothing that I could do and fortunately they bracketed the house and the next one came down on the other side. One could never completely relax. However I did have time to reflect upon the religious prodivities of the Dutch in a letter to my parents.

Extract from letter 3/12/44 Holland.

It is a very quiet nice little village and my room is at a corner of the main street just opposite the church.

Talking about churches you have never seen anything like the religiousness of the people they go to church every day (at least 50 do) and on Sunday everyone does Religeous pictures, murals, and above all busts and figures abound. I was in a room about the size of the study at home and in it were 7 religious pictures, 10 pieces of religious sculptures. Every morning and evening the whole family in every house I have been to gather to say their prayers. This lasts about 10 minutes. Along the road at frequent intervals are crucifixes, more figures and every now and again grottos with alters and edifices, all around are cherubs and figures ofChris etc.

Most impressive but one wonders whether behind all this religiousness there is much Christianity. I think there probably is, butnot all that much.

I am just listening to the king giving the home guard a pat on the back. I think it is very well deserved know few things more unpleasant than standing doing nothing for hours during the night especially when it is raining and cold, I always find it imperative to do something. Tell the people at home that I think 6 months is more likely than 30 days"

On Christmas Day I decided that my place was with my troop so I sent my Number 2 – Michael D'Arcy – to Gebroek for that day and the next which was lucky for me but not for him, since the enemy chose to attack Gebroek on the 26th. The troop of 8th Hussars who were defending the place managed to extricate themselves

With best wishes for a happy
Christmas and a victorious
New Year.

Andrews

K. Battery
Royal Horse Artillery
B. L. A.   Christmas 1944

EL ALAMEIN   TRIPOLI
MARETH   TUNIS
SALERNO   VOLTURNO

D + 1
NORMANDY
FRANCE
BELGIUM
HOLLAND

and Michael D'Arcy without too much difficulty, but Michael was slightly wounded in the action and had to be evacuated and my tank was written off. Gebroek was recaptured the following day and I applied for a new tank. We continued to occupy the place and were not attacked again.

On 9th January my turn had come up for some local leave so I and Paddy Victory had two very enjoyable nights in Brussels staying at the Palace Hotel. Although by today's standards the facilities available in Brussels would be considered primitive, they were the height of luxury to us. My letter home of 11th January describes these two days.

> *Dear Mother and Father,*
>
> *I am afraid a letter from this end is overdue, but I have just been to Brussels and I thought I would postpone it till I came back, so that I would be able to put*

229

a little more news. But before I start, I must answer some of your questions. I would very much like you to send me the knife since the one I have is not so good. You remember the argument we had about whether to take my raincoat out or not; the result of my taking it was that I wore it very little, and then a few days ago my tank went the way of all flesh, so I lost it, but I am putting in a claim for £23 (to cover what I lost on my hospital ship as well) and with that I will buy another in due time. At the moment I have ample others! The only irritating thing is that I lost my fountain pen as well, but I have bought another for 10/-, so if I lose this one the loss won't be great. Please don't try and replace it because this one is doing me quite nicely.

And so now towards my leave in Brussels. We left on the morning of the 9th and had to go quite a long way in a jeep suitably closed in to prevent draughts. The snow was quite deep and we had to use chains. We came across one bridge and then saw a notice saying bridge out of action at "such and such a reference", diversion this way. I said obviously a notice parked there in case the bridge we had first passed was broken and it was needed;- the other chap said of course and on we went. In a mile we came on a bridge out of action and had to come all the way back. Did we laugh?!

It is curious that the last leave I had in a foreign town of any size was Tripoli and I went with the same chap. Then it was sweating hot and the sun beat down on us all the way – what a change. We have

231

agreed to go on leave in Berlin together.
Every job I have had in the Regt, I have
taken over from him. He was survey
officer before me, CPO of K before me
and commanded E/F troop in K before
me. He is now adjutant – what do you
think? I don't know. His name is, very
suitable, Victory and he got an MC in
October.

Well, to continue with our Brussels leave.
We arrived at about 1 o'clock, parked our
jeep and went to our Hotel to have lunch.
The hotel is one of the best in Brussels.
Bathroom in every room, lit with neon
lights and very comfortable. In the
afternoon we went and saw the film "The
White Cliffs of Dover" and met a friend
with whom we went and had dinner, met
another friend and danced – there are
hundreds of nurses, welfare workers,

232

NAAFI, ATS, WRENs, and Lord knows what in Brussels.

Next morning we woke up at 0945 and were told that breakfast ended at 0915, but we had a good midmorning bun etc and felt as good as ever. We did a bit of shopping before lunch when I bought myself a metal watch strap and then had lunch at a hospital where our former doctor is now working. In the afternoon we walked round a bit more, and after a bath and dinner went to the Officer's club again.

This morning I bought a rather nice set of presents to the family which you will know about when you get them – sometime in the next 3 weeks. The town itself has a lot of shops and all of them have lots of things in the window but when you really get down to it, they are

233

mostly trash, or if not are incredibly expensive. You can for instance buy lace but a price a foot square costs about £5, silk stockings cost £3, and everything else on the same basis. Please don't think that what I have got cost a small fortune; it didn't. This afternoon we made our way back again.

Weather has interfered with the mails, and the only letter I found was one from Richard for which many thanks.

The snow is about 4" deep now and still coming down; last night it registered 26°F of frost; all very chilly.

Brussels itself is a well laid out town but the trams which always go in pairs (hitched together) make things very difficult and spoil it. There are some very fine buildings and wide, long, straight

234

streets with avenues of trees either side.
The main street – and by that I mean not
the one with all the shops, but the one
with all the Government buildings in it –
is about 50 yards wide. The people are
very co-operative and nice but are living
in very hard conditions, what with cold
and lack of food, clothing and transport.

Much love,
Andrew

We left Born on 17th January.

We moved a short distance north to the area of Susteren and it was very cold weather. The low temperature had affected the hydraulic system of my tank so that one tiller was inoperative. This made it nearly impossible to manoeuvre because of some quirk in the Cromwell's gearbox by which when you are in reverse the right tiller moves you in the opposite direction to what you expect. As a result if I wanted to swing twenty degrees to the right I had to do three hundred and forty degrees to the left. I had to call for help. I lost another crewmember at this time but in the changes I got a new driver – Gunner Fullaway – who was excellent and stayed with me until the end. On the 23rd we were glad to see Michael D'Arcy back again.

On the 27th January we had moved to Montfort and St Odilienburg where we had a wet and dangerous time; my letter of 27th tells something of it.

> *Dear Mother and Father,*
>
> *I am afraid this is the first letter for about 10 days but I have a real excuse. I have been extremely busy for the last 10 days and have had no opportunity of writing letters – not that I have much opportunity at the moment; but I am sure that a note, however brief, would probably improve your morale.*

You have probably heard on the news of doings on our front, and that is all I will say on the matter.

It is still very cold and there is about 2" of snow on the ground. I gather that this sort of weather goes on till late in February. We had a 2 day thaw about a week ago but that just made matters worse when it froze again.

I went and saw Alistair a little time ago. I was delighted to see that he had an M.C. What he got it for I don't know, but he is the first in his squadron to get one I think. He appeared to be in good heart, but I couldn't stay very long and it was really little but a fleeting visit.

I sent off your presents on the 18th in one parcel. I hope they arrive safely. It shouldn't take much ingenuity to find whom each one is for!

I must write to Richard and thank him for the cocoa stuff. It is very good and fills the bill exactly since one isn't always able to provide milk and sugar.

Recently we have been getting hold of some good food. We got some lovely rashers of fresh bacon and 15 eggs off some civilians two days ago, and some others gave us some bottled gooseberries and cream cheese. You must of course bear in mind that country dwellers are able to feed themselves very much better than city dwellers.

At the moment we are in a town recently captured that has suffered from a heavy raid by the RAF. It is a terrible mess; hardly a house is intact and to begin with it was difficult to tell where a road had been and where houses used to stand. It is said that 250 civilians were killed and 200 wounded and the frightful thing is that scores are still buried under the rubble. What suffering this war has brought.

The Russian news is certainly startling; their strategy is masterly, and they seem to produce the results each time.

Well that is all for now,

Much love,
Andrew

(the Alistair referred to is my cousin, Alistair Burn)

St Odilienburg is a small town with a river running through it and at this stage we occupied one bank of the river and the enemy the other. My job was to find a point in the houses from where I could observe the enemy on the other side. Not only had all the houses been badly damaged by shelling but the river had flooded and we made our way through mud and over duckboards from one house to another keeping out of view from the other side. I don't think my shooting influenced the battle very much but it helped to boost the morale of the infantry who were occupying the houses.

There was then a confusing period of activity between leaving Born and crossing the Rhine at the end of March. In this period the Battery moved seven times, usually to a position from which they could fire their guns but on two occasions into 'Harbour' positions awaiting deployment elsewhere.

The weather was cold and wet for most of the time and when it was not it was very cold with snow on the ground and hard frosts; in these conditions the tank can become an icebox since everything is metal, but we were issued with tank suits which were kapok lined with zips running right up from the foot to the shoulder. They were very effective in keeping out the cold and with the addition of good gloves we survived. The nights were usually spent in one building or another even if it had suffered some bomb damage. If you had to sleep in the open you usually dug a slit trench and had your bivvy tent above you. If you opted to sleep under the tank you had to be very careful because there had been cases in soft ground of the tank settling down and trapping the men beneath it.

Food was distributed differently from what we had been used to in the desert. Now the standard package was a fourteen man box. This was one day's ration for fourteen men, two days for seven and so on. With five men on my tank the arithmetic became rather difficult but we managed. The quality of the food was very good with quite a variety. Remarkably one of the most popular items was a tin of rice pudding, which was very creamy. We had by now moved from the old brewing

241

up in the desert and had proper burners which had to be handled carefully because they operated on petrol. There were also self-heating cans of soup, which were heated by removing a top cover, puncturing the top and lighting a wick which then ignited and heated the soup in a few minutes. These were very useful if, for instance, you were not able to leave your tank because you were on the move with the tank regiment or engaged in some activity that didn't give you a break..

On one occasion we had been very active and had not been able to stop and feed ourselves so I opened a tin of steak and kidney pudding to eat cold. I had not appreciated how cold it was; in fact it was frozen solid and I had to break off fragments of meat and suet with a chisel – not a very happy evening.

In retrospect it is surprising how well we coped with the extreme cold and wet. If you can spend all your time in the one condition and are not changing from warmth to cold you adjust to it. You sleep in your clothes and look forward to the next respite when you can have a wash and a change of clothes.

Another area of concern was handling your tank so you didn't get stuck. The Cromwell was a very manoeuvrable vehicle but would very easily get stuck in soft ground and if it did get stuck it was quite a business getting it out again. Some obstacles had to be taken slowly and carefully and others had to taken at a rush. My driver, Fullaway, was excellent at distinguishing one from the other. I got my tank stuck only once and that was when I fully realized the risk, but had to have a shot at getting to an important observation point. As soon as we felt the tracks digging in to the soft ground we stopped and in due course an Armoured Recovery Vehicle (ARV) came up and pulled us out. So by the third week in March we had moved up to the Rhine near Xanten and prepared for the river crossing and the invasion of Germany proper.

14

Advance into Germany

Arm! Arm! it is – it is the cannon's opening roar

Byron.

On 22 March we moved up towards the Rhine in preparation for the attack and spent four nights near Kapelle. On the 24th we watched an airborne attack come over our heads with scores of low flying aircraft about to discharge their load of parachutists. It must have been a nerve-wracking moment for them but they were very successful and captured all their objectives.

On one of those days I noticed an unusual staff car coming back along the road and in the back of it, fast asleep, was Winston Churchill. He wasn't going to miss the moment when, at last, British Forces were going to invade the homeland of Germany.

244

As soon as a secure bridgehead was established on the other side of the river the Engineers went to work on the bridge which was a Pontoon Bailey. They worked fast and on the morning of the 27th the Division started to move across and according to my diary I was across by 1400 hours. The actual bridge was near the town of Xanten. We were with the 5th DG at this stage and we passed through the forces who had established the bridgehead and made slow but steady progress against German tanks and 88's through Raesfeld and Weseke. Our guns were moving into two or three gun positions each day as we gradually pushed the enemy back. On one occasion I had a wonderful target of soft vehicles in front of me but I couldn't engage it because the Battery was on the move. So, in desperation, I got my signallers to load our tank gun – the 75mm and we fired it; but because we were never expected to use it, the sights had not been calibrated and all we did was to hit a pile of manure about one hundred yards away. By the time we had made some adjustments the target had moved on.

It was about this time that rocket-firing Typhoon aircraft were available to help knock out enemy armour. Artillery FOOs such as myself were the channel through which these aircraft were directed on to their targets. The drill was that as soon as our own tanks identified the target, we would range our guns on to it in the normal way using High Explosive (HE) shells. We would record that as a target and give it a name and ask for the Typhoons to engage it. The Adjutant who was near the gun position would then alert the Typhoons and tell them the location of the target and the colour of smoke we would use to identify it. The RAF would then give the Adjutant an expected time over target and he would order the guns to load with the smoke shells of the chosen colour and would be ordered to fire on the target at the right time. In this way the Typhoons would see the smoke of the expected colours picking out the target for them. Usually this worked well but on one occasion when I was calling for the aircraft they were late in arriving and the wind was blowing from the

246

enemy towards us, so that when the aircraft came over the smoke was over us and not over the target. We frantically laid out air recognition panels and prayed! Fortunately the Typhoons engaged the right targets and we were much relieved.

By 3 April 1945 we had crossed the River Ems just south of Rheine and came up against some fierce resistance near Ibbenburen where the Officer Cadets from a nearby training unit and their NCO instructors fought fanatically, holding their fire until the last minute and shooting tank commanders and their drivers through the tank slits. When snipers were located in houses these were attacked and set on fire, but the young German cadets continued firing from the burning houses until they were killed by the flames. I was with the squadron of 5th DG in those days and it was tough going.

In the end the Division decided to bypass Ibbenburen by swinging south and then east. This was entirely successful and we made fairly rapid progress towards Bremen. By 8 April I was with the 8th Hussars and we were held up in the village of Thesinghausen. (Near Kirchweyne. The hold up was due to the fact that we were now in the flood plain of the River Weser and around this village and many others a bund had been constructed to protect the village from flood. The road to the east had to rise and pass over this bund before dropping down again. Unfortunately there was a Tiger tank nicely positioned to knock out any of our tanks that put its nose over the bund.

The result was an impasse. So I went up the church tower and saw exactly where the Tiger was and had an idea that if we positioned one of our 17 pdr Anti tank guns in the churchyard and far enough back from the bund, its rounds would clear the bund but it would not expose itself to view from the Tiger. So I got the Sergeant from the A/T Battery to position his 17 pdr gun as I have described and in a straight line between the church tower and the Tiger. The Sergeant and I then went up to the tower and I started to fire using tracer so as to see where the rounds were going. We had got very

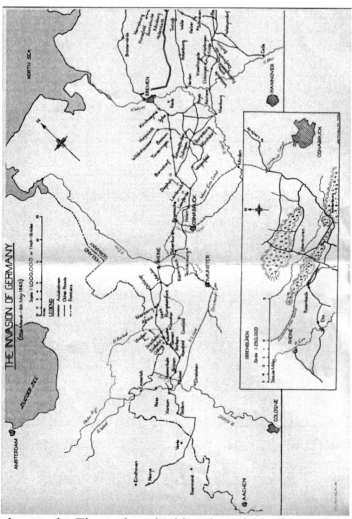

close to the Tiger when, looking through my binoculars,
I decided that I was looking straight down its gun. So I

told the Sergeant to come with me to ground level for a moment and as we reached the bottom step several rounds in quick succession came through the window we had been using.

When, after a pause, we went back up again we arrived in time to see the Tiger move away towards Bremen. I am not sure why he went as we had not hit him, but I reported this to the 8th Hussars who were able to continue their advance. They had seen the rounds go through the church window and were convinced I must be dead!

The River Weser was an obstacle in front of us and so after a few days we were moved south and crossed it at Niemburg and then moved east to Retchem and close to Fallingbostel when we liberated a POW camp. I did not personally see the camp but I was told that the 8th Hussars who liberated it found that the senior British officer was one of their own men – a Regt Sergeant Major – who had been captured some months earlier. It must have been Stalag XIB.

My letter of 20th April refers to this.

Dear Mother and Father,

Another letter at rather long interval from the last I am afraid. I hope my letter to Richard for his birthday arrived more or less on time.

Since I last wrote we have as I expect you have appreciated, been pretty busy. To begin with the weather was very unpleasant, cold and rainy, but for the last few days, it has been really warm and sunny, so warm in fact that at midday recently, the dust and heat made you think you were back in the desert again. The great thing about fighting in this sort of country is that one quite often sleeps in really comfortably houses, and sometimes in beds as good as gets at home – nearly! The last two nights, however, I have spent

251

in the open in a bivvy as many times before.

It was a great blow to hear of Roosevelt's death; it is the kind of thing one envisages but considers too frightful ever to happen. Altogether most unfortunate.

We had a most stunning episode the other day; we liberated a Prison Camp with about 8000 British prisoners and 8000 other nationalities. I spoke to the Chief British padre and he said he knew John Sinclair well and that he had gone East recently. He last saw him about a year ago, or so I gathered. Some of them had been marched from prison camps in the east nearly 600 miles away and had been fed on 2 slices of bread and some raw turnips en route. Those that hadn't been moved about were reasonably contented and said they were quite fit and well fed. I

252

gather that the really unpleasant long marches were only since the Russian push. Movements before that such as John's, were better organised. The camp itself was immense, very congested and most depressing. It consisted nearly entirely of brick built one-storey huts. Some of the officers, in fact nearly all of them, were kept in conditions that were really worse than the men's and were secluded on the grounds that too many officers were trying to escape.

Lately we drove along one of Germany's famous autobahns and was moderately impressed. The road itself is no bigger or better than one of our twin-roads; the clover leaf crossroads are good in theory but in fact the junction roads are small and cobbled with rather sharp curves. The method of flying under or over subsidiary roads is well done and comprehensive.

I hope the family's leaves work out together.

Much love,
Andrew

(John Sinclair was David's elder brother. He was taken prisoner at St Valery with the Highland Division and spent the whole war as a POW. He was released in 1945).

Although we did not know it at the time another camp in this area was liberated. This was Belsen, which became a byword for horror. Fortunately we saw nothing of it.

Some of the ground in this area was very wet with a lot of marshes and I was given the use of a Weasel which was a lightly armoured, open topped vehicle with very wide tracks which could travel over water using its tracks for propulsion or over marshy ground where its very wide tracks imposed only a very light load on the ground. In fact I was told that the load on the ground was so light that it would not set off a Teller mine. I didn't put it to the test.

On the 21st April we were across the Bremen-Hamburg autobahn and I was on high ground with a wonderful view of Elbe estuary with Hamburg just visible to the right, and Buxterhude to the left. In front of me was a railway line about three thousand yards away and several hundred feet lower. To my astonishment I saw in the distance a train travelling on the track towards Hamburg and likely to pass me in a few minutes. I hurriedly checked up with HQ as to which side was in control of Buxterhude and on being told that the enemy still held the place I decided to shoot at the train. I gave my orders to the Battery but in order to engage it they had to move their SPs and as a result had not reported ready by the time the train had arrived in front of me. I gave the order to fire when ready and the rounds came down either side of the train and about midway along its length. I quickly gave another order so that the next rounds would be ahead of the moving train when I saw that it had stopped and that the loco was uncoupling; it then hurried off towards Hamburg leaving the wagons behind. The wagons were probably loaded with ammunition and I tried to hit using one gun. But at that range the bracket of error was several hundred yards and after a few rounds I gave up. I got on to the tanks and asked them to send me up a tank to engage this target and so block the line to the enemy. It took some time for the tank to arrive but when it did I saw with some surprise that the loco had returned. Either the driver had had second thoughts or he had been given a rocket by his superior. However, the tank's second round went straight through its boiler and there was an enormous cloud of escaping steam rising up hundreds of feet.

My letter of 25th April refers to this and also to concentration camps about which we were hearing for the first time.

Dear Mother and Father,

I have had two letters and a parcel of tobacco since I last wrote. I hope you are getting my letters in as good a time as I am yours.

I am delighted to hear that John Sinclair has come back. I am writing to him as soon as I have finished this.

We are moderately static at the moment, sitting watching the Elbe as you must have gathered from the papers. I have had some amusing times. My greatest success was when I arrived on the crest of a hill and saw a train moving in the low ground in front. I engaged it with our guns which were a few thousand yards

257

behind and hit it. It blew up and turned out to be an ammunition train with no fewer than 35 trucks and it burnt for 24 hours. The engine unhooked as soon as the train was hit but came back about 3 hours later; the tanks engaged it with armour piercing and it blew up too! A great day.

Later on we tried to shoot at ships going up and down the river but couldn't do much good, because it was too great a range.

Next day we captured 500 Wrens who would otherwise have evacuated by the line which we had effectively blocked.

I had a letter from Pippa today; she appears to be in good heart

There is an awful lot in the papers these days about concentration camps that have been overrun. I am rather glad that I haven't seen them, they must be rather revolting. All we have seen, apart from the prison camp at Fallingbostel, is the ceaseless stream of refugees and slave workers tramping the roads. Every nationality is represented and it is frightful to think that some of these people have heard nothing of their families in battle torn countries for 5 years.

The prison camp was interesting. Once again there were many more Europeans (proper) to British. The British quarters were overcrowded and very dismal. We saw it on a sunny day; but what it was like in the snow and rain must be very different.

If you are thinking of sending a parcel, the usual cocoas and Nescafe etc are still 1st priority. I really need little else,

259

Much love,
Andrew

I cannot understand my reference in this letter to 500 Wrens but presumably I was referring to German Female Naval personnel. I cannot remember being personally involved!

The Pippa referred to in this letter is my younger sister who had been evacuated to the USA in 1940 with her school and had now returned to UK and joined the WRNS.

Although we were now very close to Hamburg the resistance by the enemy was still intense and for several days only slow progress was made to capture Harburg which was a few miles our side of Hamburg. I imagine that it was decided not to make an all out assault on Hamburg in view of the possibility of an early German surrender. I'd heard rumours on 2 May that Hitler had died and that the Germans had surrendered in Italy. Hamburg surrendered on 3 May and on the 4th we crossed the Elbe and passed through the city – or what remained of it. It was a miserable day and raining hard as we made our way through the ruins; and then I heard on my radio that all German forces had surrendered to 21st Army Group – the war was over. But what we were seeing was absolute devastation; the bombing of Hamburg had been intense and continuous over a long period. We were told that on more than one occasion the fires had been so fierce that a 'fire storm' ensued. As I understand it, this means that the fires were so intense that the air sucked in at ground level to feed the fire was so strong that people and cars and anything moveable was lifted up and carried into the inferno. It must have been terrifying.

I have a picture in my mind of listening to my headphones and hearing that the Germans had surrendered and seeing in front of me a cobbled street, or what remained of it, and in the centre the steel or cast iron tram line that had been blown up so as to form a curved arch twenty foot or so into the air. Beside the street was the rubble remains of demolished buildings and from the rubble there would poke a steel tube acting as a chimney, from which smoke emerged, indicating that underneath the debris people were sheltering in cellars, trying to cook or keep warm with a stove or fire. It was a sobering scene of desolation.

At the same time there was the relief that the fighting was over with two great things to celebrate – one that the free world had in the end been victorious over what we saw as evil – and that we had survived. Neither of these wonders had we been able to take for granted and although final victory had seemed certain for some time, survival could never be certain – one could always fall to a bullet on the last day of the war and we who had been at it from July 1942 to May 1945 were incredibly lucky.

We 'harboured' in the same place for the next three nights, 4th to 6th and took the opportunity to sort ourselves out a bit. Next door to where we were was a rail wagon of army clothing including sheepskin fleeces for the Russian front. I helped myself to one of these and used it for years thereafter, especially on skiing holidays or in very cold weather. Our philosophy on 'loot' was that if it was the property of German armed forces then it was fair game – you could take what you wanted. But if it was private property, you didn't take it unless it had clearly been discarded.

15

End of the War in Europe

On the 7th we moved north towards Denmark, where our objective was to secure the road/rail bridge over the Kiel Canal north of Itzehoe. I was with B Squadron of 5DG and was delayed passing through Itzehoe. In an effort to catch up I was speeding along the road when we were overtaken by a Belgian Liaison Officer, Charles du Selier, who had been with us for some time and whom I knew very well. He was in a scout car with a greater turn of speed and he made a rude sign as he passed. I told my driver to put his foot down and all 35 tons of us were speeding along at about 30 mph when we caught up the scout car at a road fork where he had stopped to read his map. I had already studied mine so went roaring past him and when we reached the bridge we drove on to it and I told my driver to switch off the engines. The engine was so hot after this high-speed chase that it wouldn't stop. We were wondering what to do next when there were two explosions from the rear of the tank. I feared that we might have some serious damage to the engine and had visions of a reprimand when one of the crew said "don't worry – it is two tins of baked beans that were too close to the exhaust cowling".

The Kiel Canal is an impressive waterway and the bridge was unusual because it was a road and rail bridge which was able to swing open for passing vessels. Swinging rail bridges are not that common and I was intrigued to study how it worked. The first operation of swinging was to tip the bridge a few inches so that one end went down and the other up. This cleared the rail tracks and the bridge was able to swing in the normal way.

Soon after we arrived a fair sized ship came down the Canal flying a Swastika. Brigadier Lyon-Smith was down at towpath level and tried to stop the ship by firing his revolver at it – not surprisingly with little effect. So, for a bit of fun, I told my driver to get out his sten gun and as the ship passed underneath us to empty his magazine into a spot close to the bridge of the vessel but not to hit anyone. This was done and the effect was instantaneous. The ship went full speed astern and came into the bank. others of our troops established what it was and my only recollection is that I managed to acquire a nice pair of military binoculars.

A small force was left to guard the bridge and the rest of us went back to Itzehoe where we heard that the Germans had accepted total surrender. The following day, 8 May, was nominated as VE Day and G Battery, which seemed to have the best accommodation, hosted a victory party in their mess. As can be imagined it was the whale of a party and when the time came to make our way back which was a matter of two or three miles there was a question as to who should drive the captured German open car which we had come in. I am not sure that I volunteered but I did find myself in the driving seat and even sober would have found it difficult to drive in darkness with no car lights along roads I did not know all that well. But we made it and I was just negotiating the last bend when I misjudged the corner and went gently into the ditch. I might have been able to explain to the sentry that it was just an unfortunate misjudgement and that six sober officers were in the car with me, if one of them hadn't taken a hunting horn from his pocket and woken the neighbourhood with a series of loud calls. I fancy that the sentry was not all that surprised.

As with most parties it is not the food or drink that really makes it go but the atmosphere. In this case the food was army rations with what extras could be acquired, the cooks were the usual mess cooks, the drink was probably local wine and our own whisky. The piano – a vital component – was in the house already and the people present were the offices of G and K Batteries – probably 20 of us altogether. We were probably pretty noisy but who was there to object? It was an all male occasion as was all our life at that time. Although we moved once or twice we remained in this area of North Germany for about two months until we moved to Berlin early in July - about which more later.

The real problem during those two months was that we did not have enough to do. There was no real role for the Army in relief and rehabilitation – this was being done by UNRRA – and training for battle was rather inappropriate when there was no likelihood of further battles. One of the initiatives at that time was by Army Bureau of Current Affairs (ABCA) who provided literature for officers to lead discussion groups on current affairs. Since a General Election in UK was in the offing a lot of this literature centred on UK Politics and plans for the 'brave new world'. Looking back on it I am sure that all the leaflets were slanted towards the left in political terms and may well have contributed to a lot of the services votes being cast for the Labour Party.

But the discussions were usually sensible and there was not much sign of political fervour.

On 27 May we had a Sports and Gala day to celebrate Hondeghem Day. K Battery had been given this Battle honour as a result of its gallant action in Belgium in 1940 when it was attacked by a powerful force of German armour. After resisting the enemy by firing their 18 pdrs over open sights until all their guns were knocked out, they withdrew in good order. Among other decorations following this action the Battery Commander received a DSO and subsequently promoted to Command the regiment (Lieutenant Colonel Rawdon Hoare) and the Battery Sergeant Major, Mr Millard, received a DCM.

One interesting detail from this period is the story that only weeks before the German attack in May 1940 an inspector of Artillery from UK came to look at the Regiment's guns. These were old 18 pdrs which dated back to World War I. After careful inspection he stamped them all 'For demonstration purposes only' and then left the Regiment to resist the enemy attack with non-operational guns. I cannot vouch for the truth of this story but, if true, it demonstrates how ill prepared the Army was in 1940.

However, back to 1945, and we set off for Berlin in the first week of July. We were to be the first British troops into Berlin and the divisional staff had a very difficult time agreeing with the Russians all the details of our journey. After a few false starts the Division finally crossed the River Elbe at Magdeburg and I was part of the advance party one day ahead of the Regiment. On reaching the city my party was directed south to Kladow which is on the west bank of the Havel Lake on the road going on south towards Potsdam. The barracks we were allocated were the Hermann Goering Barracks, fairly new and very spacious with a large central Parade Ground and Sports Centre, a small swimming pool and modern barrack blocks and officers mess in an outer circle.

Russian troops were in the process of moving out and they still had their guards at the entrance. Soon after arrival I realized that there was a second entrance to the Barracks at the south end and so I went with my Jeep to put our sign on the road. The Barrack gates were in a wood about one hundred yards from the road and the Russian guards let me through to put up the sign but when I came back they refused to let me in. They had seen me go out only a minute before but they were adamant that I couldn't come in. Language was a problem and we seemed to be getting nowhere. I remembered that a lot of American aid had been received by Russians and I hoped that this might have included Jeeps. So I pointed out to them the name WILLYS on the front of my Jeep and it worked like a charm – they recognized it as the same as on their vehicles and the gates swung open.

The condition of the Barracks was unbelievably awful. Every corridor and every room was a shambles with dirt and filth everywhere. It appeared that most of the rooms had been used as loos and, with apologies for being so explicit, rather than use paper they had used their fingers and then wiped them on the walls. I have never seen anything like it. For the next week or more we recruited local civilians, mainly women and old men, in large numbers to come in everyday with mops, buckets and brushes to clean the place up. They were all starving and were glad to earn a little money to spend on food. Watching these people coming in to clean our premises made me wonder at the turn around in fortunes over the recent months. Here were these citizens of the 'Master race' who so recently had seen themselves as Masters of the World reduced to menial service for the benefit of foreigners whom they had despised. How are the mighty fallen? But after reading about Belsen and Auschwitz I was not too sorry for them. What you sow that shall you reap!

The Barracks were very well appointed and to begin with we used the officer's mess with its large basement and skittle alley designed for competitive games and large consumption of beer. Subsequently K Battery took over a neighbouring house with just the right amount of space for about seven of us and we were very comfortable. This was the time of the General Election in UK and because of the large service vote outside the country there was a gap of about two weeks between the voting and the declaration of the result. We had a visit from Ernest Bevin – later to be a very notable Foreign Secretary. By any standards he had a very successful career starting in Bristol with his Trade Union work and his role as Minister of Labour in the war-time Cabinet, but he was hopeless at visiting troops. He didn't know what to say and my diary and letters were very uncomplimentary after his visit.

5 August 1945

"We had Ernest Bevin round here the other day to see us and have a look at our vehicles. The visit was really rather a failure; he is a most unimpressive chap and hadn't an idea of what the right

273

things to say were or how to make it seem that he was interested; with the result that he just walked round saying nothing and looking like an old publican with dropsy (my word! He is fat). His speech was short and not worth listening to and one who shook hands with him asked me afterwards if I knew what it was like with a dead, wet cod – that is what it was like. I don't think even the most ardent Socialist was a bit impressed ....

Tomorrow is August Bank holiday and I find no difficulty in recalling what happened last year; it would be amusing if I was able to bathe in the Channel on the anniversary but maybe these sort of things should be forgotten rather than have their memory perpetuated. We are having a whole holiday and the morning will be taken up with a canoe race; we

*have somewhere in the region of 10
canoes and an island that is the right size
and near at hand so the course will be
around that with a bed of weeds as an
additional hazard".*

I was fairly clueless about the British political scene and tended just to adopt my parents' viewpoint and vote for the Conservatives – not least because they were Churchill's party and he was the great hero of our victory.

Those of us who were not career soldiers were becoming bored with the pointlessness of peacetime soldiering and were straining every nerve to get out of the Army and begin our life's work – whatever that was. I was busy trying to confirm my place for Cambridge in October 1946 and pulling all strings to ensure that I got out of the Army in time to take up my place. Meanwhile we made the most of what facilities were available – we sailed boats on the Havel and we recovered some neighbouring tennis courts and even found a squash court which we managed to repair and bring into use. There was plenty of German labour to be had but they all wanted to be paid in cigarettes. Economists have subsequently studied this strange phenomenon of cigarettes taking over from cash as the main medium of exchange. I never found out whether anyone smoked them in the end, I suspect not.

We had no trouble with the local population and had dealings with them only when we wanted them to do something for us. They were fairly cowed and this is not all that surprising. The difficult problem that we did have was trying to hold the ring between them and the Russians. The war on the Eastern Front had been brutal in the extreme, as anyone who has read the account of the Battle of Stalingrad knows. The Russians and the Germans seemed to regard each other as vermin and acted accordingly. Within a few days of arriving we discovered that each night in our area groups of drunken Russian soldiers were terrorizing the local German population. They would barge into a house, rape the women, break up the furniture and set fire to it as they left. Very soon we were having to send out patrols of our troops at intervals during the night to prevent these outrages. It is not difficult to imagine what our troops thought about giving up their time to protect their late enemies from their late allies. But our men were part of a disciplined force and did what they were commanded to do.

On 15 July 1945 delegates started to arrive for the Potsdam Conference; most of them arrived by air at Gatow airport and from there travelled down the road past our Barracks to Potsdam. We were told that the first VIP would not be passing our gates until 9pm, but when I was passing our main gate at 5pm I found a queue of lorries held up and not being allowed on the road to take the troops on their normal evening outing to Berlin. I found the road lined with Russian troops with a pair of men every five yards or so. I went out and asked to be directed to their officer and was shown someone wearing the badge of rank of a Major in the Russian

Army. We managed to converse in broken German and I asked him why he was not allowing our vehicles on to the road. He said his orders were 'no vehicles' even though there was four hours before the first VIP was expected. I asked him who was his superior officer and he said his Colonel was at the road junction fifty yards away. So I said I would go and talk to him. He said "No, if you walk down the road you will be shot". I then said that if that were the case he, the Major, would take me down to see the Colonel. He said, "No, if I leave this tree, I will be shot". At this point I gave up. Majors in the Russian Army do not seem to have much delegated authority.

I have one other story about the Russians, which I believe to be true. The four zone Commanders in Berlin – Russian, French, American and British – used to meet regularly to co-ordinate their activities and on this occasion the British staff car was damaged by some wild, careless driving by a Russian driver. When the Brigadier emerged from their meeting the British driver pointed out the damage while the Russian Brigadier was listening. The Russian then summoned the culprit, questioned him, and subsequently he was taken behind a building and summarily shot. They were not easy people to understand.

Berlin itself was a mess. Possibly not quite as devastated as Hamburg but nearly so. The Charlottenburger Chaussee runs through a park up to the Brandenburg Gate and the trees in this part looked like something out of a surrealist painting by Salvador Dali. They had limbs blown off and shattered trunks. We couldn't travel far beyond the Brandenburg Gate because this was the Russian zone but I went far enough to see the remains of Hitler's underground bunker and shell of the Hotel Adler. It was now just two months since he had committed suicide there and the Russians had fought their way in. We were glad not to have been involved in the storming of Berlin – it must have been very rough.

16

Victory Parade in Berlin

"The tumult and the shouting dies
The captains of the kings depart
Still stands thine ancient sacrifice
An humble and a contrite heart
Lord of hosts, be with us yet,
Lest we forget – Lest we forget"
Kipling.

On 21st July the Great Victory Parade took place and Winston Churchill took the salute. By some quirk of Army tradition the RHA when on parade with their guns take pride of place at the right of the line, so 3rd RHA were first and we came second and after us came Hussars, Guards etc. Churchill was in the first half-track as he travelled down the line of troops and with him were Brooke, Montgomery and our Divisional Commander LO Lyne. After them came the other distinguished guests, which included, to the best of my belief, Attlee, Truman, Stalin, de Gaulle and other world figures. Roosevelt had died earlier in the year so Truman was now President of USA

It was a memorable occasion and a real celebration of victory by parading in the centre of Germany's capital city. After the parade Churchill came to open officially an Other Ranks Club which was to be called 'The Winston' and in doing so made the following speech:

> *"Soldiers of the 7th Armoured Division. I am delighted to be able to open this Club and I shall always consider it a great honour that it should be named after me.*

> *I have, not for the first time, had the pleasure of seeing your troops march past, and this brings back to my mind a great many moving incidents in these last, long, fierce years.*

Now, here in Berlin, I find you all established in this great centre, from which, as from a volcano, fire and smoke and poison fumes have erupted all over Europe twice in a generation. And in bygone times also German fury has been let loose on her neighbours, and now it is we who have our place in the occupation of this country.

I feel that I can go so far as to ask Field Marshal Montgomery to signalise this happy event of the Great Victory Parade we have had today by giving a whole holiday to all the troops in Berlin and I hope, Field Marshal, that you can accommodate this to operational and other necessities.

Now I have only a word more to say about the Desert Rats. They were the first to begin, the 11th Hussars were in action in the desert in 1940 and ever since you have kept marching steadily forward on the long road to victory. Through so many countries and changing scenes you have fought your way.

It is not without emotion that I can express to you what I feel about the Desert Rats.

Dear Desert Rats! May your glory ever shine! May your laurels never fade! May the memory of this glorious pilgrimage of war, which you have made from Alamein, via the Baltic, to Berlin, never die! It is a march unsurpassed through all the story of war as far as my reading of history leads me to believe. May the fathers long tell the children about this tale. May you all feel that in following your great ancestors you have accomplished something which has done good to the whole world; which has raised the honour of your own country and

283

which every man has a right to be proud of".

You can imagine that we all felt pretty chuffed at hearing these words from so great a man as Churchill and we all came out a bit broader around the chest!

However, one must keep a sense of proportion and 7th Armoured were not the only division of whom this could be said. I am thinking of other great Divisions such as 50th (Tyne and Tees) and 51st (Highland) and there must be others who had a history of continuous battle every bit as distinguished as 7th Armoured. What I think happened is that the spin doctors of the day wanted a formation that would catch the public attention and raise morale generally. They chose us for several reasons, one – because the name Desert Rats was an evocative one; second – because we were in it right from the beginning; and third – because an Armoured Division gives a more powerful impression of thrusting power than does an Infantry Division.

The Army as a whole emerged from the war with a good reputation and great things were achieved. We were all grateful that we did not have to fight a battle like Stalingrad – compared with that we were just playing at it!

It is interesting to look back on our relationships with the German civilians in those very stressful days of 45/46. In the countries that the Germans occupied in the war years – and I am thinking of Italy, France, Belgium, Holland – the jackboot was the order of the day and we heard lots of stories of brutality even if not actual murder. In Holland where we spent several months we were, of course, welcomed with open arms. I say "of course" because there have been many years of friendship between the Dutch and the British and we were able to relieve some of the worst effects of famine – they were really very hungry in Holland in 1944/45. We were not sure what to expect when we crossed the Rhine and I was interested to see how our troops would relate to the Germans. In the event we found the

Germans cowed and nervous but not unfriendly; they, of course, were not sure what to expect. I was amazed to see how friendly our troops were to the civilians – especially to the children. If there was any criticism to make it would be that they were too friendly. As soon as the war was over an edict came down from on high that there was to be 'NO FRATERNISATION'. We were instructed to keep our distance and treat them as defeated enemy and not as long lost brethren. It never worked – you could not stop the troops making friends of the people they met and after a few months the edict was quietly rescinded. In this brutal world of death and destruction in which we lived and operated it was heart-warming to see the reverse side of hatred. On the back of one lorry I saw "GET WISE – FRATERNISE"!

I had one embarrassing episode on our way up to Bremen. When the time came to stop for the night I was in my tank, separated from the Battery, and chose a small farmhouse standing on its own undamaged. The occupants were very helpful when I said the five if us wanted to sleep the night there. They made two rooms available and offered us what facilities they had. I told my driver to park as close to the building as possible so that from the air it might look like a lean-to shed rather than a tank. Next morning we packed up and made our farewells, thanking the farmer for his help. Unfortunately the driver tried to make too sharp a turn from his parked position and in a tank if the front moves one way, the back moves the other, and this is what happened. It took away the corner of the wall and half the house collapsed. It was difficult just to say "sorry" and drive off, but this is what we had to do!

On 30th August we moved from the Barracks at Kladow to the Olympic Stadium site, nearer the centre of Berlin. This whole complex had been built for the 1936 Olympic Games when Hitler wanted to show off his New Germany to the world. He particularly wanted Germany to win more gold medals than any other country and was very angry when the famous Jesse Owens walked away with so many of the golds that he coveted. He was angry not only because Owens was American but because he was black and to Hitler blacks were an inferior race. The accommodation for us was comfortable and we were much nearer the centre of Berlin than the rest of the British forces. Quite a lot of entertaining went on, -- cocktail parties and dinner parties and I seem to remember being a guest at an 11th Hussars dinner party when Anthony Eden was present – a very formal affair with strict protocol.

As far as the forces were concerned it was a predominantly male population but there were one or two organizations of mixed sexes. One of the difficulties was finding a place where you could take a girl out to dinner and the only place I found was the YWCA. I remember one evening when I and our second in command Peter Gillett took out two Wrens to this place and had a very enjoyable but very proper evening.

On 5th October we left Berlin and travelled back to Schleswig Holstein - this time to Heide north west of Itzehoe and onto the western coast of the peninsula

288

facing the North Sea. This was a time when there was a lot of posting from and to the Regiment. Many of the older men were leaving to be demobilised and others were coming in to take their place. Our Battery Commander, Geoffrey Armitage, was one of those who left and I found myself commanding the Battery for several weeks. I cannot remember whether or not I put up a Major's badges of rank, but I was doing a Major's job. The main leisure activity was wild fowling. We were close to the shore and there were a lot of wild geese and ducks to shoot at. I did a lot of shooting at but not very much shooting down!

Eventually on 18th December my turn to go arrived. Anyone who was due for demob within a year had to leave in case the Regiment was sent overseas again. Since I fell into that category I had to go. I had been with the Regiment for four years and two months and was sad to leave it. They had been the most active and important four years of my life and I was a very different man from the callow Subaltern who had joined them in October 1941. It had been a rough and violent way in which to find one's feet but I had been with the same people mostly and great friendships and respect had been established. I left with a feeling that a difficult job had been well done by the Regiment of which I had been a part.

I was posted to 13th (HAC) RHA who were near Kiel. They were little more than a holding Regiment at that time with about half their usual strength of officers and other ranks. My Battery Commander, Philip Kinnersely, was also from Bristol and we spent many happy hours riding horses around the countryside. We organized a Christmas party for some of the local children, which seemed to go down well but it was difficult for me because I hadn't had time to get to know any of the people.

My main occupation at that time was getting down to my books of mathematics and science and trying to prepare for an Engineering degree course – hopefully in the following October. I also got hold of (via my father at home) all the volumes of Gibbon's 'Decline and Fall of the Roman Empire'. This is a huge work but I gradually worked my way through it and am glad I did. My real incentive was that there was a great gap in my knowledge of history between the death of the Roman Emperor Trajan in about 100AD and the Norman Invasion in 1066. I had read in the paper about Wavell being asked who were his favourite generals in history and one of his choices was Belisarius and I had never even heard of him, so I thought I had better find out (He was, in fact, the Commander of the Army under the Emperor Justinian).

I applied to go on an Education Course of the Rhine Army at Gottingen and surprisingly got a very early acceptance and travelled to Gottingen via Hanover on 8 January 1946.

17

Home at Last

The month I had at Gottingen was very pleasant. The course was organized for just such people as myself who had the necessary school qualifications but wanted to be brought up to speed for further study – in my case a degree course. The accommodation was simple but perfectly adequate and the place itself charming. Gottingen is famous mainly for its university, which was founded in 1734 by George II of England who was also, at that time, Elector of Hanover. It is also well known for its Mannequin Pis statue in the main square which is of a boy very obviously having a pee. We spent most of the day in lectures or private study and at weekends went into the nearby Harz Mountains and either skied or skated. The evenings were usually spent

292

in the local Gasthaus with steins of the local beer interspersed with occasional glasses of Benedictine. It wasn't too bad a life.

On 27 January I came back from skiing to find a telegram from home congratulating me on receiving the MC. This was a complete surprise to me and I had never considered the possibility and with great forbearance I waited six days for confirmation before sewing the ribbon on to my battledress and walking out a bit taller! It was odd that the authorities did not notify recipients but expected them to read it in the London Gazette. It happened to coincide with the announcement of my father's CBE so the family had a good week.

There are two types of gallantry award – the 'immediate', which is given for one conspicuous act of gallantry and is awarded very soon after the event – on the battlefield as it were. The other type is given at the end of a campaign. I believe that each Regiment or Battalion is told by the Army Commander (or whoever) how many DSOs, MCs, MMs, DCMs, etc they may award and this will obviously vary with the amount of good work the regiment has done. Normally the DSO is given to the formation Commander if his unit has excelled itself. The DCM is an other ranks award and is frequently given to warrant officers or to other ranks who have nearly qualified for the VC. I was lucky to have been given one of the 5th RHA allocations and it may well have been influenced by good reports from the tanks or infantry, which I had supported and helped. Whichever way it was, it was a great honour. There were so many awards of this type that there could not be investitures for us all and I received mine by post with a nice letter signed personally by the King. The other medals which 'came up with the rations' were the 1939/45 Star, the Africa Star (8th Army), the Italy Star, the NW Europe Star and the Victory Medal. I expect that I was also qualified to wear the Defence Medal but since this was primarily intended for those in UK who had carried out any war work I decided not to apply for it.

I tried to get taken on as an instructor at Gottingen but there was too much of a queue. They told me that I might be lucky in March. So at the end of March I made my way back to Kiel; Where I found that the Regiment was breaking up and I was posted to 4th RHA in Kiel".

4th RHA was a Regiment that had had a similar war to 5th RHA but was going through the same experience of losing a lot of its men and receiving an intake of new ones like myself. We were in a barracks not far from the centre of Kiel and I was first posted to F (Sphinx) Battery and then a few weeks later was appointed Adjutant to the Regiment which was an interesting job and gave me something positive to do. The Adjutant is the Chief Staff Officer of the Regiment and is a Captain. He is in charge of all administration and all orders from the Commanding Officer (Lt. Col) go out over the Adj's signature. There is therefore a very close liaison between the CO and the Adjutant. In action the Adj co-ordinates the Regiment's activities where this is necessary. If for instance all three Batteries are called upon to engage the same target at the same time or join with other Divisional Artillery then the Adj is the man who does the co-ordinating.

Out of action it is more mundane. I remember one awkward problem at Kiel. The CO – Richard Goodbody – for whom I had great respect, left and was replaced by a less impressive man. One evening he was crossing the parade ground and heard a shemozzle at the main gates. Very unwisely he went to investigate himself when he should have sent someone else to do it. There were some very drunk sergeants one of whom called him a f***ing sh*tbag. The CO insisted that he be Court Martialled but since the CO was the chief witness he could not arrange the court-martial himself so I had to organize it through a neighbouring Regiment and it all became very complicated.

A court martial is, of course, a court of law and as Adjutant I had to arrange for all the witnesses for the prosecution and ensure that the accused also had someone to defend him. It was difficult enough on one's own premises but arranging it to take place with another Regiment organising the prosecution was more difficult. I cannot remember whether the Sergeant got off or not – I think probably not. I am sure our CO felt rather foolish.

One of the Officers who joined 4th RHA at about the same time as I did was John Butler who had served with the Surrey and Sussex Yeomanry in Africa and Italy and had been awarded a DSO as a subaltern. We found ourselves doing a lot of things together including a skiing holiday in Chamonix in March. We learnt that a grateful French Government were offering free skiing holidays for British Army Officers and we leapt at the opportunity. We spent two days in Paris on the way there and I remember having a meal and drink at the magnificent Rothschild house in the Rue Fauborg, which is, I believe, now the British Embassy. I hadn't seen Paris for fifteen years and with the first signs of spring it was a magical place. We saw the Folies Bergeres and visited Montmartres and absorbed the beauty of the city and its parks – mercifully undamaged by war. The skiing at Chamonix was great fun even if not very skilful; it was very icy and we both came back with bruises.

Back at Kiel our main leisure activities were sailing and pike fishing. There were a lot of small lakes in the vicinity and with rudimentary equipment, mainly a spoon bait constructed from a sawn-off mess spoon and a fearsome hook, we fished for pike and were usually successful. After one afternoon's fishing John suggested that we call in on a Red Cross Team to see a girl he knew called June Norbury. This we did but found her confined to her room with 'flu. In this way I met for the first time the girl I married eighteen months later and with whom I will be celebrating our fifty-fifth wedding anniversary later this year. In return I introduced John to my younger sister and they were married three months before us.

The Red Cross Team was a fairly small one – only about ten of them – whose main occupation at this time was trying to help the large number of 'Displaced Persons' (DPs) in the Kiel area. Over the last few years Hitler had forcibly moved thousands of young people from the countries of central Europe to Germany to provide labour for their factories and once the war was over these people found themselves abandoned and homeless with no knowledge of whether their families had survived the war or not. They were living in hutted camps and added complications included the number of single mothers and babies. There was a certain amount of social life including tennis and the Red Cross team was one of the few women's organizations in an otherwise male environment.

Most of us were directing our attention to getting out of the Army as soon as possible and you could either opt for PYTHON (acronym of something unknown) which gave you four weeks leave but then the risk of being posted to another unit or LILOP (leave in Lieu of Python) which gave you a straight four weeks leave and back again to the same unit. I decided to opt for the first but, if possible, to be incommunicado over a critical period of two weeks when they might post me elsewhere. The plan was to go on a walking tour in Switzerland. Unfortunately the Swiss frontier was virtually closed at this time and the only way Army personnel could get a visa was if they had a close relation living in Switzerland. I managed to get two copies of the form you needed if you had a close relation and discovered that it had to be signed by a Brigadier (General Staff) at Rhine Army HQ. I reasoned that if I could persuade another brigadier to sign the form the frontier guards would not notice the difference, So I tried the old trick of getting a local Brigadier whom I knew quite well to sign the forms at a drinks party and it worked like a charm. John Crosthwaite and I entered

Switzerland near Basle and no one asked us any questions.

We left our luggage and our uniforms at an hotel in Lausanne, took a train to Les Diablerets and walked first to Gstaad; we then intended to walk over the Hahnenmoos to Adelboden, but even in early June there was too much snow. We walked down to Frutigen and then back up to Kandersteg where we had a lovely few days. There were hardly any tourists about and we were nearly the only guests at our hotel.

From there we walked up to the Gemmi Pass from where you look down on Leukerbad nearly three thousand feet below; the escarpment is vertical at this point but there was a path which took you down to Leukerbad. It was like going down three thousand feet by stairs. Despite the fact that we were fairly fit, our knees were knocking by the time we reached the bottom. Nowadays, of course, there is a telepherique which takes you down in five minutes. We found Leukerbad too rich and unfriendly and the hotels didn't want to know. So we knocked their dust from our shoes and went on to a more welcoming place. From there it was down into the valley and a train back to Lausanne and then back to England.

This is the end of this story but I must have one more paragraph to describe the moment when we left the hotel in Lausanne to start our walking tour. As soon as we emerged on to the streets dressed in comfortable shorts and with rucksacks on our backs, I felt acutely uncomfortable, underdressed and out of place. For the last four years I had been wearing the uniform of an Army Officer and we had been fighting our way through many countries where the civilian population had to dance to our tune; without being in the least bit overbearing we had nevertheless been calling the shots. I found myself one of these civilians and it took a little time to get used to it. It dawned on me that now I had to learn to be a nobody again and start form the bottom. A salutary lesson!

Epilogue

"And I wager it is as old to you

As the story of Adam and Eve".

Browning.

My two years at Cambridge were a joy after six years as a soldier and the peace of the College Gardens and normal life as a human being again were wonderful.

We felt very old at 24 to be starting as undergraduates but were quite prepared to work hard in order to catch up and not miss out on the jobs that would be on offer. The Dons also found it strange dealing with undergraduates who, in many cases, had been commanding Regiments or naval ships. In my case I found out only years later that my Director of Studies for my Engineering Degree was 18 months younger than I was.

There was more social life than we had had over the last four years but that was not difficult since it had been nearly zero. But in 1946 Cambridge was still predominantly male – not many colleges allowed girls to be members nor even to be on the premises later than a ridiculously early hour.

There were only two Ladies Colleges at that time – Newnham and Girton – and one or two associated establishments such as Homerton. Apart from this other restrictions were fairly archaic. Gowns had to be worn on nearly all occasions and college gates were closed at 11 pm. If you were out later than this you had to climb in over the wall. In the case of Pembroke there was an easy access from Tennis Court Road where a convenient lamppost enabled one to climb onto and over the wall. Some years later the local authority removed this lamppost and the college objected on the grounds that it was a convenience to the young men!

There was no basin in my room in college but I had a freestanding bowl in its own stand and I would fetch water from along the passage and "bedmaker" would empty it when he/she cleaned the room. The nearest bath was down two floors to ground level and across to New Court and down one level. There had been a proposal to install bathrooms closer to the rooms but it was turned down on the basis "that the young men are up at college for only 10 weeks"!

I got into trouble once for visiting the University Library to see the Librarian about an overdue book without wearing a gown and this resulted in a letter from him to my tutor.

But generally speaking we put up with these petty restrictions and played the game. The college authorities realised that they were dealing with mature people.

You had to scratch around to find a girl to take to London for the Varsity match and as for the May Ball that required an importation from outside. For the 1947 May Ball – Pembroke's Sexcentenary – I got in touch with June Norbury whom I had met near Kiel a year or more before and found that she was in Brazil but she nevertheless managed to come to the Ball and that led on to our wedding in 1948. John Butler from 4 RHA was at Christ's College at the same time reading English and my younger sister, Philippa, was his partner at the May Ball and subsequently for life.

Those two years leave wonderful memories of punts on the river and also at Hemingford Green, madrigals by the bridge in King's College, squash, tennis, Rugger, and innumerable bicycles. We recharged our batteries.

The rest of my working life – making stainless steel in Sheffield followed by a move to Imperial Tobacco Co in Bristol in 1953 – has been satisfying and fulfilling. I have been particularly happy to live in the house where I spent my childhood. Our family expanded and this book is dedicated to our eighteen grandchildren.

Various thoughts come to mind as I look back after 60 years. I suppose the first is that I was extremely lucky not only to survive but also to have done such exciting things at a relatively young age in the company of men I liked and admired. At that sort of age one needs to do something exciting and find out how much you are able to rely on yourself and be independent. For this reason I am very much in favour of a 'gap year' between school and university or school and apprenticeship. Not only does this meet the need to learn independence but it prevents having a feeling later on of having missed out on travel or exciting experience. Another thought in retrospect is that it gave me a wonderful respect for my fellow soldiers. At a time when horrible atrocities were commonplace, the British soldier never betrayed his innate decency and put up with danger and discomfort with admirable restraint. It sounds rather trite, but I became very proud to be British.

Since leaving the Regiment in 1945 my connection with it has been limited to the annual reunion lunch in London and the occasional dinner. But June 1994 saw the 50th anniversary of D Day and a week later the citizens of Villers Bocage chose to dedicate a memorial to those allied troops who had died there 50 years before and to honour the few British Regiments who had fought there. I was asked to be one of two representatives of 5 RHA and it was a moving occasion. It was particularly generous of the village to commemorate the action in this way when one remembers that three weeks later the whole village was completely destroyed by the RAF after due warning had been given – all the inhabitants left before the bombing.

And lastly, following on from this I felt that whatever accusations were flying around about why the war was fought and what was done, this country had acquitted itself with honour and courage and we could safely feel that we occupied the high moral ground. You could not ask for more than that.

Glossary

Army Formations

Army Group	Commanded by Field Marshal
Army	Full General
Corps	Lt General
Divisions	Major General
Brigades	Brigadier
Regiments or Battalions	Lieutenant Colonel
Companies, Squadrons or Batteries	Major
Platoons, Troops etc.	Captain

British 7th Armoured Division: the Desert Rats

11th Hussars, Prince Albert's Own (Cherry Pickers)

8th King's Royal Irish Hussars

1st and 5th Royal Tank Regiments

Queen's Infantry Brigade

1/5th Queens Royal Surrey

1/6th Queens Bermondsey

1/7th Queens Southwark

4th County of London Yeomanry (the Sharpshooters)

1st Battalion of the Rifle Brigade

3rd and 5th Regiments of the Royal Horse Artillery

The Norfolk Yeomanry 75th Anti-Tank Regiment Royal Artillery

The 5th Inniskilling Dragoon Guards (the Skins)

Allied Tanks

Cromwell: 75mm gun, 2 machine-guns, 70mm (later 100mm) armour, 30 tons, 35mph

Valentine: 2-pdr or 6-pdr gun, 25 tons, 25mph

Sherman M4: 75mm gun plus 2 machine guns, 75mm frontal armour, 32 tons, 24mph

Sherman 'Firefly': 17pdr plus 1 machine gun. 75mm frontal armour, 32 tons, 24mph

Honey M3/5: light reconnaissance tank. 37mm gun, 40 mph.

German Tanks

Panzer Mark IV: 75mm gun, 2 machine-guns, 30 tons, 80mm max armour

Panther Long 75mm gun, 2 machine guns, 45 tons, 80-120mm frontal armour

Jagpanther: 88mm gun, 1 machine gun, 80mm frontal armour

Tiger: 88mm gun that could penetrate 100mm frontal armour at 3000 yards, 54 tons

Acronyms etc.

ACV	Armoured Control Vehicle
ADC	Aide-de-Camp
ARV	Armoured Recovery Vehicle
CO	Commanding Officer
CO2	2nd in Command
CPO	Command Post Officer
CRA (Brig)	Commander Royal Artillery
DF	Defensive Fire
DUKW	Amphibious Personnel Carrier
ENSA	Entertainment National Services Association
FOO	Forward Observation Officer
LST	Landing Ship-Tank
MO	Medical Officer

NCO	Non-Commissioned Officer
OCTU	Officer Cadet Training Unit
OP	Observation Point
OR	Other Rank (i.e. not commissioned)
POW	Prisoner of War
QuarterMaster	Officer in charge of Supplies
RASC	Royal Army Service Corps
RSO	Regimental Survey Officer
Subaltern	1st Lieutenant or 2nd Lieutenant
UNRRA	United Nations Relief and Rehabilitation Administration
VE Day	Victory in Europe Day
VI	Pilotless German Bomber
WO	War Office
WVS	Women's Voluntary Services

YWCA   Young Women's Christian Association